"A 90-day devotional you will want to read in one sitting! Written with the wit and whimsy Jami Amerine is known for, and with the heart and passion for helping others embrace the freedom and grace she has found, *90 Days to Stress-Free* offers readers encouragement, inspiration, laughter and a blueprint for living with less worry and more grace. This is a book that will touch your heart, and one that you will want to gift to others."

JENNIFER MARSHALL BLEAKLEY, author of *Joey,*
Project Solomon, and the Pawverbs devotional series

"I love any book by Jami because I know it will be packed with hard-won wisdom and life-changing encouragement. And this book stayed the course! If you feel let down by the world and stressed out by everyday living, let Jami lead you to find hope to believe things can be different. Finally. Soak in the wisdom of this page-turner and learn to live empowered and stress-free."

CAREY SCOTT, author, speaker, and life coach

"Life can be messy. We all need a remodel and an upgrade when we get weary and peace gets harder and harder to find. In Jami Amerine's new book, *90 Days to Stress-Free*, she takes us on a journey of renovation . . . of our beliefs about Jesus and the mistaken beliefs we have about ourselves. Meditating over ninety days of devotions, you'll feel like you're sitting at her kitchen table, letting her down-to-earth wisdom inspire you, encourage you, and remind you that, in the eyes of Jesus, *you're much more than a fixer-upper.* Let her words and wisdom affirm to you that we're all holy works in progress."

KATE BATTISTELLI, author of *The God Dare* and
Growing Great Kids

T0006650

90
Days to
Stress~Free
Renovating the House
That Worry Built

Jami Amerine
Foreword by Tracy M. Steel

KREGEL
PUBLICATIONS

To Kim,
look how we
turned out!

Foreword

As an interior designer, I am hired for a specific purpose: to bring beauty and function to the space my client occupies. What starts as a vision in my head is cut to specification and upholstered. The furnishings are shipped, placed, and hung per my direction. At the end of our initial planning meeting, my client usually says something like, "Just make it work, Tracy."

Just make it work.

Do I care about their needs? Do I long to please them? Heavens, yes. But to show them every detail would overwhelm them, and I can't place a desk where they suggest if it violates an egress code. I don't expect my client to foresee issues like this. But I am the designer responsible. If I say no to a client, it's for a reason.

Just make it work.

So I do.

Looking back, most of my clients rested in who I was as a designer because of my credentials and my character. Our relationships were pleasant ones.

Unfortunately, other clients tried to run the show, which would create delays and cause the final space to not live up to its potential in either looks or utility. Our stress levels often spiked, causing frustration and disagreement.

Even though I am no longer a working designer, I am still a worry-prone daughter of God. In times of stress, I wonder if God might not be able to "just make it work."

Perhaps you can relate! I know my amazing friend and sister in the faith Jami Amerine can.

Here is what I know and have witnessed in Jami's heart and mind as I've watched her follow after our Master Designer with everything she has: Jami is letting God just make it work for her and through her.

In this book she shares how God has helped her release her past and present stresses. My friend is more at peace, more secure, and more joyful than I've ever seen her. And you can be too.

So I hope you'll unplug from Pinterest and put those home-decor magazines aside as you settle into your favorite chair and reflect on the biblical passages within this book. Jesus Christ came to this earth, died a brutal death upon a cross, and rose again from the dead to renovate us in the most holistic sense. The work of a human decorator will never be able to restore you like our Master Designer can.

I pray you will apply the tools and wisdom Jami shares on the following pages.

Stress doesn't have to be the dominant resident of your heart and mind anymore. Allow God to be the only One going forward. For he is busy making it work in your life and in mine.

TRACY M. STEEL

speaker, mentor, author of *A Redesigned Life: Uncovering God's Purpose When Life Doesn't Go as Planned*

Introduction

Hello, friend.

Welcome to your renovation to stress-free!

Such a bold proclamation, I know.

It was during the composition of my third and fourth books, *Well, Girl* and *Rest, Girl*, that I was determined to uncover the root of all my worries.

My mental residence, my mind, was decorated just as my physical home was—with decor any good Jesus girl would choose. There was WWJD garb and ornate crosses on the walls. My sound system piped "Amazing Grace" into every room, and my prayer chair was warmed and lit by a classy yet chic Tiffany lamp on an antique side table that had followed me since college. I liked to sit there because it was pretty and quiet.

But if I am to be brutally honest, which you will find I am, despite all the religious paraphernalia in my life, I still struggled with stress and strife. Usually my only hope to reduce my stress was to keep on keeping on despite my misery.

Back then my heart song was, "In this life, you will have struggles. Jesus overcame them. And I give up."

My "religious" habits, my beliefs about my wrongdoings, and the message of eternal life were conflicting with my tangible experiences. All the good news I knew in my head wasn't making a difference in my heart and life. I clung to the Scriptures "I can do all things" and "Lord! Help my unbelief!" The clash of exclamations was like a tacky, pleather avocado-green couch and tomatillo-red shag carpet—a mess of retro-industrial-eclectic style with splashes of Pharisee.

Gross indeed.

And being the way I am, I spoke up and asked anyone who would listen, "Why does the Bible promise peace, joy, patience, and abundance, but I am so worried, so afraid, so broken?"

What is the other promise? Oh yes! Ask, seek, find.

I didn't find my answer through wise friendships. It was not any of the dozens of religions I tried. The problem was simply that I was living in the squalor of limited, kind-of, maybe, mostly on Sundays faith and professing rote religious words that were making me bust at the seams of need, want, and growth. No wonder chaos ensued.

My struggles went beyond what my limited faith was able to handle. So I went to the house of science. You can call the house of science whatever medical, psychological, or, as in my case, secular study you'd like. I discovered I can often affect my outcome by thinking positively. At

first investigating my faith through a scientific lens felt . . . haunted. And then it felt curious. And then I took my findings to a friend, a wise spiritual gal who is my creative match. I sheepishly reported my discoveries. She pondered and said, "Can you back it up with Scripture?"

And I could. So I did.

I pointed to verses about giving "thanks in all circumstances" (1 Thessalonians 5:18), how good people focus on good things and then produce good (Luke 6:45), and how anxiety is eased by focusing on thanking God (Philippians 4:6).

Now my friend and I live stress-free, as do my husband, our children, and our friends.

Want to know how we did it? Come on in and I'll show you. In fact, one of my spiritual gifts is hospitality. So pull up a chair. Grab a pen, maybe a journal, get cozy, and let me tell you all about this wonderful way to believe, for real, and live in the abundance of peace we were promised. The world will let you down, but Christ and the results of his sacrifice are real.

Here's the thing. We aren't just cleaning out a closet or rearranging the living room. This is a gut job. We just keep digging at our spiritual foundation and moving walls in an effort to know how to get from messed to blessed. Lucky us.

God gave you the blueprint. Even better? He gave you the Holy Spirit, who is your personal helper, and Jesus, who not only built the world but is right next to you helping you renovate your life. God is exactly who he says he is. Greater, he called the job of renovating your life "finished." Do you hear that? God is so certain of your transformation that it's as if it has already happened.

So let's do this! I love a remodel, a new home build, a fresh coat of paint, or a recovered chair so very much. And I am giddy with joy to take this internal renovation journey with you! My husband, Justin, and I have spent the majority of our thirty-plus years (and counting) together making a living in construction management, design, and building. Who would have ever thought that those experiences would directly link to the freedom we were promised?

I propose that is the problem—we try to DIY our faith journey. We deconstruct, try it from this religion or that, fret, chase, and struggle to get to and finally get God so we can have that most coveted promise of peace.

Friend, there is no wait for what is already done. There is no struggle to obtain that which is already yours. We are here now.

Welcome home.

Jesus be all over you.

Love,
Jamie

SECTION ONE
Glass, Wood, and the Rock

DAY 1

Knock, Knock

*Ask and it will be given to you; seek and
you will find; knock and the door will
be opened to you.*

MATTHEW 7:7

I used to say today's Scripture in my sleep. Ask and it will be given to you. Seek and you will find. Knock and the door will be opened to you. Sounds so simple: There's something you want—in this case stress-free living—so you knock on God's door to ask for it. And . . . voilà. There it is!

In fact, there's a sign hanging on the entrance to your transformation:

Everything in my life as a follower of Jesus Christ is easy.

Except it doesn't feel that way, does it? Perhaps your thought is:

That's easy for her to say—she doesn't know what I'm up against!

Well yeah, but Paul said . . . or Moses said . . . or Pastor Davis said . . .

Or . . . whatever.

And you would be right—it is easy for me to say. In fact, I say it all the time.

And yup, I don't know your trials.

But I am so bold because *I get it.* There 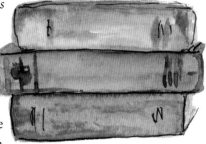 are a lot of words in religion and church, sometimes even the Bible, that feel like doom, gloom, and wrath. But Jesus said come. We are here to let Jesus be Jesus and do his thing.

So here we stand at his door to transformation, to freedom, to peace.

You alone decide whether to venture inside. But!

Are you deciding?

Will you knock?

My initial response to this question was, "Of course I am the one deciding. I'm the one who had the thought, *I'm going to knock*." And the next thing that popped into my head was, "So why are you still here, standing at the door and not knocking?"

And I didn't know.

We are inundated with information. We live in a world of 5G, and we function in a society that often feels more cyber than real. And I have come to understand that so many things were telling me what to think and do. My Google Maps could get me where I needed to go. Facebook tailored my feed to confirm my likes and those who opposed them. This tragedy on the news or that story a coworker shared, which I believed had no liability to my physical person, elevated my heart rate and left me in a tailspin.

And that was when I knew for sure I was still standing outside the door to freedom, waiting for someone else to tell me when it was safe to venture into the unknown.

I bet you can identify. We hop from conviction to condemnation and from this belief to that judgment of others. We borrow trouble from people on the other side of the globe, allowing ourselves to be agitated and broken but unchanged. We watch thirty seconds of video blurbs that challenge us but don't engage us in self-discovery.

So we will start at the beginning.

You and I will choose to walk up to the door, and we will look with our own eyes and truly decide for ourselves.

The door to freedom is heavy, solid wood—the grain carries a sense of warmth and sturdiness. The dark stain hints at reclusion or a retreat. And your perfect helper is on the other side.

Imagine yourself standing at a door. Do you see it? It doesn't matter what else is in front of you or behind you. All that matters is who is standing on the other side. I am not here to force you to open the door.

This is about you actively saying, writing, chanting, singing—whatever *you* do to initiate your belief—and then participating in your choice to pursue peace.

And then, you decide. Will you knock?

I'll give you a minute.

Good choice.

THE FINISHING TOUCH

Lord, my God and Friend, I am actively deciding to believe that peace is possible. I am choosing to knock. I am choosing to ask for help. Thank you for hearing and answering me. Thank you for the clarity of knowing your voice. Amen.

DAY 2

Cracks in the Foundation?

They are like a man building a house, who dug down deep and laid the foundation on rock. When a flood came, the torrent struck that house but could not shake it, because it was well built.

LUKE 6:48

In 2017 we moved from our ranch in the very dry, extremely windy Abilene, Texas, to our Houston house just in time for Hurricane Harvey. We love Houston. And before you guffaw, let me tell you, Houston is fabulous. If you have never been and have only seen photos, you might be thinking, *Doesn't all of Texas just look like an episode of the Road Runner cartoon, with an occasional motor home and random skyscraper?*

No, Wile E. Coyote, it does not.

We live in a forest of towering pines on a huge lake. I have never seen such remarkable skies. The clouds remind me of explosive mountains, constantly morphing. We are minutes from some of the finest dining in the world, as well as great shopping, shows, and museums. We are an hour from the beach and forty-five minutes from some of the most fantastic camping to be found.

As I compose this,

it is six days until Christmas, and it is sixty degrees and sunny. The projected forecast for Christmas Day is a crisp fifty-two degrees. Sophie, our youngest daughter, flew in from New York yesterday. Luke, our third oldest, will fly home from Hawaii on Christmas Eve. This means all four of our eldest children and their spouses will be joining Justin, me, and our two youngest boys, Sam and Charlie, for Christmas. I am one happy girl.

Still, no matter how fragrant my descriptions, you might be thinking, *I need a white Christmas.* Or *She failed to mention Houston's rumored standstill traffic or the 599 percent humidity or the stifling 110 degree August afternoons.* And I have my responses, but I am not here to convince you to move to Texas.

I am just here to point out that you are you. Your foundation is not my foundation. My beliefs are no threat to your beliefs, and yours are no threat to mine. If you despise all things Lone Star State, I can still love it. My bumper sticker may command you not to mess with my state, but I am too busy to do anything about it.

Just like I'm not worried whether or not you love Texas, Jesus isn't threatened by your doubts or concerns. He can't be deconstructed. You don't need to try to figure out whether or not he'll come through.

His nature was confirmed when he died on the cross and then rose again. Unlike your preference for places other than Texas, who he is is fact.

If we're struggling with Jesus, it's because we're dealing with misunderstandings, and we have foundation work we need to attend to.

With any renovation, we must first make sure the structure is secure before we do anything else. After we get the underbelly cleaned up, we rebuild the way the structure functions on the seamless, crack-free foundation.

We have to teach the subconscious, or what I call the heart-head, how to trust something new. We can say that Jesus is our strong foundation. But years of difficult real-life experience combined with limiting beliefs and questions about God have the heart-head desperate to truly believe something but struggling to. Our rehearsed words about lack, want, and suffering have taught our minds to disbelieve Jesus's faithfulness.

We have so much information and experience that bury truth, like debris crusted over old wood flooring. But if we scrape those floors, if we acknowledge and dig for proof of Jesus's claims that he is our good helper, we will see for ourselves that God is indeed our strong foundation, and we can build something new from there.

Today I invite you to write out a list of things that you know are true of God. Now *choose* to actively feel and believe these promises. Write out today's Scripture (or another that talks about God's plan for you). Feel the sturdiness of the words, and rest in the comfort of being seen, heard, and known.

THE FINISHING TOUCH

Jesus, I want to truly know and experience you. Open my eyes to who you truly are, and help me enjoy your peace and abundance from the ground up! Amen.

DAY 3

Framing

But test them all;
hold on to what is good.

1 THESSALONIANS 5:21

I like to be in the know. If I'm going to have to replace my water heater, I want to know why it can't be repaired, when I can take a hot bath, and how to light the pilot. The desire to know all things has been detrimental to my religions but has caused exponential growth in my faith and has fueled life-changing discoveries about God and myself.

Unfortunately, this exploration has caused me to lose a few companions along the way. These losses were usually sad but only came when I could no longer subscribe to what was being taught by authority figures and culture.

What is the difference between blindly accepting what an authority says and building our own faith?

Words don't teach.

Death to the wordsmith? No, we need words. They are the framework for what we seek to know. However, just like a house needs a frame *and* siding as well as Sheetrock and plaster, we need more than words. We need words that lead to fulfillment of God's promises.

Allow me to ask you, how are your walls coming? Are they strong and functional? Are they beautiful? Do they do what they're supposed to do? Or are you constantly plastering them with duct tape and praying they don't cave in on you?

If it's the latter, why do you continue to prop up something that isn't working well? God promises abundant life (John 10:10). Are you unhappy or stressed because of what you are being taught, or are you ready to experience the rogue freedom of learning directly from God and his Word?

The challenge is that your subconscious is comfortable with the old duct-taping way. Your mind warns you not to try building something new because it might be hard. Part of the subconscious's job is to make you stay with familiarity—this is the reason even *good* changes cause stress. Change, even as minor as paint color, causes the subconscious to go on high alert. The subconscious, the heart-head, wants everything to stay the same, where it knows you're safe. Modification takes work, and the heart-head will quickly talk you out of a life remodel.

I use the analogy of dieting and exercise to explain this. With your conscious mind, you decide to wake up an hour earlier than normal tomorrow and walk two miles and then make a smoothie for breakfast. You set your alarm, lay out your sneakers, and go to sleep chanting, "This time I'm doing it!"

At 5:30 a.m. your alarm goes off, and the subconscious—well-rested and ready for ease and pancakes—says, *The bed is so warm. Start next Monday.* Suddenly that "I can do all things" attitude is only alert enough to hit the Snooze button nine more times. Later the subconscious will be there to chastise you—*I knew you wouldn't do it.*

Good grief.

The heart-head is talking and learning from what you feel, good or bad. It doesn't take much for the subconscious to equate trying new things with feeling bad when you fail.

In the same way we hit the Snooze button, we go to our church buildings on Sunday morning and the heart-head learns, *That was church. Good teaching, friends, family, potluck—all good stuff.*

But outside those walls are real troubles. Mortgages, layoffs, pandemics, stray kiddos, and politics. You may quote Scriptures, but if the church doesn't add strength to your life's building, then it is okay to acknowledge those feelings. That's when you take your thoughts captive and move into the new, roomier space that Jesus bought and paid for once and for all.

Jesus is stable and sturdy as ever. Even if your church isn't prepared to answer your legitimate concerns and questions, Jesus welcomes honest seekers.

Today I invite you to consider: What changes do you want to see in your foundational relationship with Jesus? What parts of your faith are permanent within the structure of your beliefs? What walls or barriers need to be moved or reconsidered? Are there faith upgrades you'd like to research?

I know it's hard because the heart-head only knows what it has learned from the experience of comfy feelings. Write a note to your heart-head about how much good is on the other side of trusting Jesus. Your subconscious is listening to a lot of noise. Tell it a renovation story as if it has already come! Intentionally align the words of your mouth with the thoughts of your heart-head.

Look how roomy that is!

THE FINISHING TOUCH

Jesus, I want to bust out of the old and make way for the new. Open my eyes to the possibilities. Calm my heart-head as I venture into the new way of seeking you. Amen.

DAY 4

The Rough In

But understand this: If the owner of the house had known at what time of night the thief was coming, he would have kept watch and would not have let his house be broken into.

MATTHEW 24:43

In construction, specifically plumbing, electrical, and HVAC (heating, ventilation, and air-conditioning), the initial stage is called the rough in. If you have never walked through a home in this state, I'll tell you that it looks like a framed house with wires, pipes, and ductwork poking through the wooden studs. It is progress on the project, but it isn't much to look at.

Here I am among a heap of wood, concrete, and gadgets that don't interest me. Who just wants to fluff pillows?

I'm not lazy; I'm just not a mechanical kind of gal. I want to pick paint colors and stew over fabric swatches. However, we all know you have to plug in the lamp before you turn it on, and that plug better be hooked up.

But as pedestrian as they are, the rough-in stage technicalities are necessary to build the rest of the home. And that goes for building a stress-free life too.

In order to depend on your faith, you best know what the details and facts are.

With our conscious minds, we profess our belief in the fact that Jesus died on the cross to pay for the things we've done wrong. We say that we believe we are free from the consequences of our sinful choices. However, what's going on behind the scenes? Back behind the Sheetrock, what do you *really* believe? Do you know? You may answer, "I believe God is good and Jesus died for my sins." But is your heart-head (the machine that not only reminds you to breathe, eat, and yawn but also registers stress) in agreement with the words of your mouth?

If with your mouth you profess, "God is good. He will help me," but your heart-head is humming behind the Sheetrock, "God didn't help you get that promotion or heal your brother-in-law's cancer," that thought is your *real* belief.

Your subconscious doesn't miss a thing. The subconscious saw an alarming TikTok that combats your belief about God and what you thought you knew for sure. Then the subconscious mind, with its easily swayed convictions and feel-good-now demands, created a genius image tearing down your faith and trust in God.

The bad news is the heart-head can't tell the difference between perceived threats and real ones. So that horrifying news clip you watch from the safe comfort of your living room? Your heart-head thinks you are there scaling walls, begging for escape. With your conscious mind you are sitting, watching television to unwind. Meanwhile, your heart-head is screaming, "Get up and run, dummy!"

Simultaneously, the subconscious releases the hormone hounds of real panic—adrenaline and cortisol. Who knew after an early morning, a quick stint at the gym, a Zoom call, an angry coworker, grocery shopping, traffic, dinner, bath time, story time, and cleaning up after the dog, you would now also have to battle the Taliban!

You don't, really. That's the good news.

The even better news is that you don't have to pay attention to the TikTok dissing God either.

Instead we can choose to look at the mess, disaster, or malady and say or write out what we know to be true and then choose to feel safe, protected, and loved. We can recognize that the wires are crossed and the plumbing is backing up in the sink simply because we didn't know to prepare. But now that we know where the threat is coming from, we can plug in the power of truth.

Today I invite you to stop and identify your feelings in any given instance, and then tell the heart-head what you know and need it to understand. This practice retrains the mind to know the difference between an actual leak behind the fridge and a runaway ice cube that has melted on the floor.

If, like me, you know a lot of Scripture, what Scripture verses come to mind when you stop and identify the feeling and then apply a scriptural promise to the emotion? Can't think of one? Go use the internet for something good and search for Scripture verses about God's love and security. This is a practice in activating the subconscious in the discovery of your why. Why do you believe something? How is it serving your peace? And what does Jesus have to say about it? When we get the practice of looking for truth down, it becomes an epic part of a real belief, which equates to living stress-free.

Lucky you! Plug that lamp into the true power source.

THE FINISHING TOUCH

Lord, open my mind to the endless goodness I have doubted.
Help me look beyond the mess and see
what you see. Amen.

Mind Makeover

We've discussed what's going on behind the walls of our minds. What've you noticed going on behind the scenes of the statements you profess?

As a way to help train your mind to see good things, choose one of the statements below and use it as a breath prayer. Meditate on the statement. Inhale and exhale through the words as they run through your mind. This is an excellent way to allow your heart-head to feel what you're trying to learn instead of arguing for or against what you've been taught.

I find rest in the foundation that is Jesus.

Jesus is the One I trust with my worries.

Thank you, Lord—I do not doubt your tender-loving care.

You are peace and goodness. Help me feel you.

DAY 6

Swivel-Chair Jesus

Let us then approach God's throne of grace with confidence, so that we may receive mercy and find grace to help us in our time of need.

HEBREWS 4:16

D r. Andrew Farley, speaker and teacher of all things real freedom, explains many believers' faulty understanding of God's judgment of them. Pastor Farley asks if the listener believes in a swivel-chair Jesus—where Jesus is turned toward us when we are "good" and away from us when we are "bad."[1]

This concept has stuck with me. This spinning is exactly what I believed Jesus did. Monitoring and keeping a running record of my good and bad deeds. Say we took in a foster placement, check! He's facing toward me. But when we turned away a foster placement because we were sick with the flu, the Jesus of my mind and beliefs swung his chair away from me, too disgusted to gaze upon me with his divine eyes.

Beloved, that is not the seat of the Christ. There is no separation we can fabricate to keep us from the love and care of God. You cannot earn his favor—it was already bought and paid for. Were you to have to pay back the work of the cross, it would no longer be a sacrifice—it would be a purchase. If you were to try to earn it with your good deeds and ninja volunteer moves, it would become a wage. And you are not strong enough, good enough, or wealthy enough to pay the price to gain God's love.

The promises of Jesus are true. You are seen, heard, and known. You were not created to be in a heap of stress and terror. You were created in the image of God (Genesis 1:27).

Furthermore, God tells us to ask for the things he's promised and then believe as if we have received it, and it will be given to us (Mark 11:24).

So what is the problem?

Experience.

Our past experiences are the problem. Our brains remember and react to hard or dangerous scenarios, and if you've had your share of them, or like me just have a fantastic imagination, your brain is spring-loaded to release stress chemicals and fear-based responses, which bounce around in the same space. Then your self-talk ends up sounding like this: "You should worry about this, but you really should have more faith in Jesus. Also, this seems like it is really, really awful. And . . . Jesus."

I know it may sound too good to be true that we don't have to feel this way. But hold on—you'll soon see that the fulfillment of God's promises is plausible *and* that it's possible to think, speak, and live in the promised freedom. We can find grace in our time of need.

The tiresome, costly worry-work is the incompleteness of religion. Grace, which makes no logical sense and makes no apologies for the claim it holds over you, is free. The chair that Jesus sits on needs no swivel bar or wheels. He doesn't need a desk pad to protect the streets of gold. He is comfortably seated with nothing but love as his measuring stick, which has no beginning and no end.

Today consider your religion (as opposed to your faith). Consider what is required of you in religion versus what you experience in the intimacy of relationship with Jesus. Ask yourself, How would Jesus meet with me in this moment? Would he be sitting formally behind a desk, a scowl upon his face? Probably not. You have a sit-on-the-floor kind of relationship with him. When you compare what you think God requires with what he actually asks for, you'll see that certain beliefs about what is expected of you came from man. What Jesus offers is in the heavenlies.

He will never turn from you in disappointment. If there are rollers on his chair, he only pulls himself nearer to you in a swift and easy motion. Nothing . . . no, nothing can separate you from him (Romans 8:35–39). He will not accuse you or ever turn away from you. There's no beginning, no end to love just as there is no beginning or end to him.

THE FINISHING TOUCH
Lord, thank you for wisdom and understanding. Thank you for your protective care and for never turning from me.
I trust and I believe you. Amen.

DAY 7

Glass and Light

*In him was life, and that life was
the light of all mankind.*

JOHN 1:4

A glass front door and glass cabinet doors say a lot about a home and the homeowner. Glass goes hand in hand with light and is indicative of transparent authenticity. Glass and light are easy ways to open up a space visually. Natural light pouring through huge windows makes it easier to work, visit, read, or just sit and stare.

Glass that is etched, colored, embossed and glass with texture, patterns, and shapes still allow light, albeit in a more obscured way. Stained glass or frosted windows allow natural light into the home while adding privacy and light play.

I can already hear some of you saying, "I can't have glass in my cabinet doors or open shelving. No one needs to see all that."

Yeah, we all have things that we would rather stay hidden.

Let's be honest though. While dark spaces with no natural light may be a cozy place to watch a movie, nap, or sleep, living your entire life under forced fluorescent blue light is a bit of a torturous endeavor . . . much like trying to do anything under the heavy weight of failure.

The word *sin* is taken from the Hebrew word *chata*. *Chata* was not a law-based word. It simply meant a failure to meet a goal.[2]

In the Ten Commandments God sets up the standards for perfection, and they're listed in two parts. The first five commandments are failures in our relationship with God, and the second five are failures in our relationships with humanity.

The subconscious (the heart-head that we already learned stores the memories and images of past strife) takes those commandments and transforms them into a finger-shaking taskmaster who makes you feel guilty for looking at them funny. And suddenly instead of living in the freedom of God's promised grace, we're constantly talking about shoulds and shouldn'ts. Then as we try to keep up, the subconscious keeps shoveling on more woulds and wouldn'ts in an effort to be satisfied with something, anything about ourselves.

When we focus on our sin and failure, we're shutting ourselves up in a dark, dingy dungeon.

But there's good news. Not only did God send Jesus to fulfill those Ten Commandments, Jesus paid the price for all our wrong choices, then swung the door open, scrubbed the windows to our soul clean, and let the light in. Further, we are not in trouble for our messy cabinets or the fingerprints on our front door. Fretting over failure is not who we are anymore. Stress often comes as we try to process the contradictions between being "saved, free, and peaceable" (the truth) and "don't you dare step out of line, dreadful sinner" (our self-made dungeon).

Jesus's words "free indeed" (John 8:36) have to match the experiences we are having. If the subconscious can't make this connection, worry and struggle are the consequence.

After our yes to Jesus, we no longer have to live in the throes of strife. We are no longer in the dank prison of the law-bound. Jesus is the light that leads us out. When our focus is strictly on the truth of God's freedom, the light within us grows stronger and more vibrant.

The heart of the gospel, the good news, was . . . well, good. There are no buts. You are loved. Pure and simple. You can't earn it, pay it back, or lose it. When moved by the light of Jesus, darkness disappears.

What is the difference? Try it today.

Turn off the light and do an everyday task, like brushing your hair or tying your shoe. Now turn the light on and try it again. Isn't it easier in the light?

Every time you're tempted to count your transgressions, stop. Remember that you are in the light. Then rehearse a promise of God and move on with your day in the light and freedom of Jesus.

THE FINISHING TOUCH

Jesus, I want to experience more and more of your light. The less stress I put up as a blackout curtain, the more I, too, will be filled with the light of your kingdom. Bring your kingdom on earth as it is in heaven. Amen.

DAY 8

Live Edge

He has filled him with the Spirit of God . . .
with knowledge and with all kinds of skills . . . to cut and set stones, to
work in wood and to engage in all kinds of artistic crafts.

EXODUS 35:31, 33

A live-edge slab is beautiful piece of hardwood with an unfinished edge. The boundary of the wood slab is not altered by wood-working machinery or hand tools. The unworked end of the slab and the furniture then has the primal characteristics of the tree it originated from—both its shape and its bark. The slab can be included in a variety of settings and spaces for your home, office, or business.

Milled butcher block or wide-plank benches and dining, coffee, and end tables are the most popular, but pops of live-edge decor can be sneaked into just about any room to add character, warmth, and texture.

I love the addition of live-edge treatments in nearly every design

style. The rings, knots, and waves of stained or epoxied wood give depth and character to otherwise rote, manufactured particle-board pieces. And this is the root of today's lesson.

Jesus lives. He is alive and dwells in you (Ephesians 3:17). Look closely at that. Jesus *dwells* in you. What does this mean? For me, for years it meant that Jesus was lurking around waiting to see what awful thing I would do next. However, once I took the time to let Jesus shine light on that, he exposed my misbeliefs, and oh, friend, the things I have seen.

Let's head back to the live edge for a minute. The fanfare with live edge began inside of settlers' log cabins when they came to start new lives and build their homes in the New World. Unable to bring much with them on the high seas, families needed practical yet functional furnishings. The hurried arrival and need for housing forced the "nesters" from another land to get creative. So trees were sawn into single unfinished slabs. The slabs were then used to build basic furniture, such as tabletops and work-spaces. And this worked great. But then the processes improved, and carpenters sawed everything straight and clean and perfectly uniform until we, with our modern advances and habitual practices, have neglected to look at the natural intricacies of individual cuts of wood.

Do you see it? We've structured our lives around uniform right and wrong, giving no space to God's magnificent, unpredictable grace and our individual relationships with him.

God is more than a simple fabricated piece sitting in one corner. He is not a decorative knickknack that simply adds to the aesthetic. He moves in with all his glorious live edges and takes up all the attention and space. There is no partial residence with Jesus.

Oh, but love. He more than barely meets our functional need. He is beauty, function, and style. He is adoration, joy, and peace. And as I close today's devotion, let's also acknowledge a great irony. Jesus is the One who was laid in a rugged manger and then suffered on a cruel wooden cross for our sins so that they were no longer our burden. And he continues to guide us in the ways of the Father, who sent him.

I invite you to experience him. Look! There! In that tree or bench. That coffee table or four-poster bed. It is more than a place to set your cup or lay your weary head. It is detail, beauty, familiarity, and comfort. It is given to you by a loving God who yearns to enter your life in ways unique to you and your needs. Where will you see his presence today? What wonders will you discover?

If you're anything like me, the more you see, the more you'll realize Jesus is more than the edge of the piece. He is the entirety.

THE FINISHING TOUCH

Jesus, I trust and believe you. Today when I see a piece of wood, a tree, or a mantel with a live edge, I want to stop and look more closely. Not at its function but the intricate design of its creation. Thank you for coming into my life in the exact way I need you. Amen.

DAY 9

Of the Hill

But he who is joined to the Lord
becomes one spirit with him.

1 CORINTHIANS 6:17 ESV

Famed architect Frank Lloyd Wright was known for having nature in his designs. Wright didn't simply "use" nature to enhance his work—nature was the foundation of his work. "No house should be on a hill or on anything. It should be *of* the hill, belonging to it. Hill and house should live together, each the happier for the other."[3]

From experience I can say that we have weak faith because our lives are built *on* a hill (hey there, thanks for hanging out with me) rather than *of* the hill (let's bind ourselves together with Christ). It's important to remember that Scripture not only calls Jesus the Rock but also says he's a cornerstone—the one piece that holds the building together, the piece that bears the weight of it all. Basically he should be what grounds us *and* holds us together.

The question is, why do we as the Christ-following species struggle with connecting to Christ? Why does tangible, miraculous change often evade us?

I think the answer is that we all have a knickknack brand of faith that doesn't advance us beyond a timid, kind-of-hopeful faith to a "bulldoze that wall and make room for a banquet hall with a dance floor and karaoke stage" belief. Instead of truly welcoming Jesus into our heart-homes, we put our faith in money, a political alignment, a job, and the rules, none of which work.

The perfect place to start is saying thank you to Jesus for loving you perfectly and without contingencies. There is no "I love you . . . but." There's no legalese to your restoration project, and the work is guaranteed. You are not "kind of saved." The perfect sacrifice of Jesus dismantles the strife of sin that once motivated and terrified. The blood worked, and it is finished (John 19:30). Doesn't that sound like a love rock you can build your life into?

And yet . . . here we are, hanging by rusty nails. Which brings us to our second step: acknowledging that it is easier to hang our hats on a hook that we can touch and see. However, I am compelled to inquire, if you hired a roofer to fix your roof, would you hire a second roofer in case the first one didn't fulfill his commitment? When you order new mini blinds, the next day do you order more in case the first set doesn't show up? If we pour a foundation deep into the rock, why on earth would we build our house somewhere else?

Habitually worrying that God won't save you is living on top of the hill, ready to make an escape if it doesn't all work out. Somewhere along

the way we believed in the past, rehashing mistakes and losses and imagining the worst-case scenario, instead of believing that Jesus loves us with no strings attached. This is the essence of worry—belief in the probability of termites, crooked contractors, and black mold, which eat away our relationships, our confidence, and our peace of mind.

However, we have enlisted the greatest help, the Stone—the solid, impenetrable help. One might argue, "But God let me down before." And I would rebut, "Did he though?" Or is it possible that you abandoned your rock-solid foundation and built your house on top of a bit of lovely sand (the belief that money or that guy or that job will save me)?

Shoog, only one foundation was built by a professional redeemer. If I focus, in this moment I am in complete unison with my Creator. The things that happened two seconds ago are gone. And I don't know precisely what will happen in fifteen minutes.

So right now, I can acknowledge God as my rock.

Now it is your turn. Sit in the now. Breathe for a minute. What do you feel? Is God part of you or a standby? Are there other things you're relying on instead of him? Shift your focus away from those unreliable foundations. Now breathe out the negative associations with their failure and breathe in God's stability. Maybe say some of the breath prayers from day 5's Mind Makeover. Be one with who he is. Write about and *feel* the connection!

THE FINISHING TOUCH

Jesus, open my eyes to the interference of worldly answers. Help me think with rock-solid clarity, giving thanks that you are not just a part of the design—you are of me. Thank you. Amen.

DAY 10

Mind Makeover

We've discussed the essence of our life in Christ, the raw nature of his light in our lives, and the stony and sturdy path he guides us on simply because that is who he is.

- *What have you noticed throughout your days in focusing on him instead of sin, culture, religion, and the world's interference?*

Focusing on Jesus, letting Jesus be who he is, and choosing to trust him are going to usher us into the arms of real peace. As we have acknowledged with our conscious and subconscious heart-head that our focus is easily swayed as we search for solutions to our problems, we are simultaneously cleaning up this problem with choosing to trust. I can't wait for you to practice living in this life-changing mode. Over the next few days, any time you spot wood, glass, or rock, practice some Mind Makeover statements. Here are a few possibilities:

❀ I am a loved child of God.

❀ Jesus, thank you for your grace.

❀ Lord, I do not doubt your tender-loving care.

❀ Thank you for helping me feel you.

SECTION TWO
Scarlet, Burgundy, and Rose

Red Doors, Walls, and Letters

We see that God has carefully placed each part of the body right where he wanted it.

1 Corinthians 12:18 msg

Not afraid to stand out? A red door might be the door for you! If you never turn away a guest or hide under the dining room table if someone rings the doorbell, red is your color. In Scottish tradition, when a homeowner paid off their mortgage, they would paint their front door red. Because no mortgage means, party! In early American history, a red door was a symbol to weary travelers that the home was welcoming.

But for many people, my husband included, the color red is too flashy and might just be the source of a migraine. This is why driving my bright-red convertible is not for him.

In our first custom home, I painted the dining room tomatillo red. Years later when selling the home to move to another, several potential buyers said they couldn't live in a house with red walls.

Alas, some people will never think the way I think.

But it's critical to acknowledge that our preferences and personalities do not advance us toward nor separate us from God's love. In fact, he not only created us with specific talents and desires but also designed our individual preferences.

And here's the fact: all believers are covered in red.

Let me explain.

Red blood over the door of your home during the Jewish Passover marked your home as "safe." In the New Testament, red letters portray the words of Jesus in many Bible translations, symbolizing the blood that was shed for our redemption.

The red letters written on your hearts mean you are God's child, no matter what you look or sound like.

Our worship of him might be bold and robust. Or it might be contemplative and quiet. We may be doused in #Jesus garb and have an entire wall dedicated to his death and resurrection. Or we might search for God in the peace and quiet of a springtime forest. Our doors and walls may be painted bold reds, and our bumpers may be decked out in WWJD and "Honk if You Believe" stickers. While it's nice to belong, louder or quieter doesn't always mean better or worse. It simply is part of our design.

And it's all just fine until it slips into feeling like we're doing this faith thing better than someone else.

Many stresses are laid to rest when we no longer believe all Christians must think and behave identically. Think of the freedom here. If someone looks at me and says, "Too bold!" I can point to the blood of

Christ. And if someone looks at my friend and says, "Too quiet!" she can point to that same freeing blood.

We cannot be responsible for how others feel or behave, but with God's guidance, we can be responsible for what is right and good for us. Christ the Redeemer came to save all, and for this we have grounds not only to release judgment of ourselves and others but to give thanks.

In fact, let's write it out. Grab a paper and a pen.

Write: God, thank you for making me unique. Thank you for the freedom to be who I am. I am free indeed.

And if you're feeling especially spicy, underline that last part in bright red.

THE FINISHING TOUCH

Lord God, I give thanks to you, the creator of all. I love how uniquely and wonderfully made I am. Thank you for your careful contemplation of the world. You are indeed a Master Designer. Give me eyes to see your grand design and all the ways you move in each of us. Amen.

DAY 12

In the Dry

*Let us hold tightly without wavering to
the hope we affirm, for God can
be trusted to keep his promise.*

HEBREWS 10:23 NLT

The phrase "in the dry" refers to the construction stage when the home can no longer be impacted by wet weather. It means exterior doors have been installed, the windows are in place and working, and the roof is ready for inspection. It means the interior is protected from the outside forces, raging storms, and rough patches. If you hired someone to renovate your home, you would expect they'd have it "in the dry" before you started arranging furniture.

Sounds like the basic expectation of any home, right? So let me ask you, are you dry? And I don't mean literally. I mean, is your interior—your heart-head—dry? Or are the storms of life flooding your interior?

Just because you are used to needing extra buckets for leaking stress and worry doesn't mean that it is what you must continue to expect. In fact, I urge you to *stop* expecting stress.

There is power in expecting Jesus to show up. And yes, I know the word *expectation* sounds forward. How dare we demand Jesus answer us? And I get it. Especially since we can get hung up on Scripture's use of the word *hope* when talking about our expectations of God.

You might hope your roof of sanity will hold up one more year under the raging winds, but if it doesn't, you will get wet. Many of us have said or heard the words, "I am putting my hope in Jesus." However, if there is a steady drip, drip, drip on your head because "I am still hoping, but the couch is soaked," hope will turn to doubt. Doubt is an emotion fostered by the downpour of stress hormones, lack, and the warning, "If you don't do something, you'll be under water."

That thought combines with your flooded family room to create your actual belief—God isn't coming. It's nearly impossible to foster faith when reality soaks you in doubt. We don't have to look far to find examples of events that don't seem compatible with an all-powerful, loving God.

But biblical hope carries the idea of endurance (1 Thessalonians 1:3), unswerving promise fulfillment (Hebrews 10:23), and renewed strength (Isaiah 40:31). Fulfillment of God's promises will take place on God's timeline. And the time might not be now.

But the time is coming. And in the meantime, we can expect and experience the feelings of being "in the dry" by choosing to believe and then communicating that to our heart-heads through our words and actions.

I suggest we get bolder in our professions and anticipate dryness from the rising flood waters. How, you ask? Through our senses. We must feel and experience the good sensations of expectation and anticipation so that we might identify them and use them to close up the holes in our faith.

Unfortunately, many of us have accepted our saturated state and believe worry is an unchangeable part of who we are.

In an effort to perfectly align the words of our mouths with the deep beliefs in our heart-head, we must start paying attention to our surroundings, to what we are saying, thinking, hearing, and feeling and experience more of what we expect from our faith walk.

That doesn't mean we snap our fingers and life is miraculously as we hope. It's much more like the process of getting a literal structure in the dry. Each step brings us closer to the completed house. Perhaps the roof repairs start by going to counseling, and filling in the walls looks like trying some meds. But in the meantime, we can purposefully look for progress, be thankful, and then feel the feelings of expectation for the next step and the next.

Feel the anticipation and wonder of the miraculous!

Okay, today's challenge might make you feel way out of your comfort zone, which is great! Write the words "Jesus, I expect . . ." Remember, he loves you and he likes you. Expectation can be expressed in adoration and gratitude.

I'll go first:

Jesus, I expect to see you in everything on my morning walk.

Jesus, I expect to have a great day.

Be cognizant of your feelings. Often if we write a word we don't regularly use, it invokes new feelings. Great! Write what you feel. Finish your thoughts. Hear what you are saying.

Nice job!

THE FINISHING TOUCH

I expect miracles, Lord! I offer you my whole heart, expecting not only that you will answer but also that you already have. I will rest in your timing and believe as if I have received. I expect my faith to grow in leaps and bounds! Amen.

DAY 13

Rooster on a Red Tin Roof

Look, I am sending you out as sheep among wolves.
So be as shrewd as snakes and harmless as doves.

MATTHEW 10:16 NLT

O f the characters Justin and I have encountered in our "Flip it, move it, paint it, demo it from the ground up" ventures, one is most memorable. Bill Baxter, may he rest in peace, was a unique individual, with a mouthful of gums and few teeth, armed with a crafty toolbox of exclusive and oddly appropriate construction truisms.

My favorite: "That fits like socks on a rooster!" This was in reference to stripped threads, impossibly cramped ductwork, loaded-down work trucks, and tight-fitting tool belts. However, I found a new use for it.

Us.

For the believers, the brethren in Christ, worry and strife are not supposed to be part of who we are, and the fit is tight and itchy—like socks on a rooster. Stress is a bad fit.

In the last reading we talked about how our incorrect expectations cause stress. And we talked about how God wants us to expect good things. But there's something more here.

Remember that we are covered in Jesus's red blood. We aren't meant to look like everyone else. Seeing a red roof is uncommon in neighborhoods with HOAs. But a red roof, much like a red front door, makes a bold statement.

We are bold statements, and God asks us to take our grand expectations to the rooftops. I would like to suggest that we the Christ followers have gotten wishy-washy in our declarations. Maybe it's simply because we have talked ourselves out of the miraculous with everyday, plain-Jane safe coverings.

We have forgotten to feel bold and unstoppable, only whispering to ourselves and a few close companions, "I can do all things through Christ" (Philippians 4:13 NKJV). I recognize this behavior because I did it too.

We experience a miracle or see God in our lives, and we barely acknowledge, "That was a God thing." I won't speak for you, but I will ask you what I ask myself: Why are we timid about declaring a miracle? In our need to not sound like a religious whack-a-doo, or priggish, we stifle our thanksgiving, negating the good feelings of bold faith. We are actually harming our audience and ourselves.

So I am here to say, shout it out! Be bold, and not in an icky, judgmental way but in the fragrant, rose-colored praise of expectation and gratitude! In an effort to mind the HOA (religion, politics, social correctness), we've tried to look like the world and still follow Christ, while not causing offense, and, oh dear, no wonder we're under stress.

I'm not suggesting that you be offensive for offensiveness's sake. If a red roof is going to get you run out of your neighborhood, it might not be the place for it. After all, I'm pretty sure the God who sent fire from heaven (see 1 Kings 18) or walked on water (Matthew 14) can take care of himself. Being argumentative typically doesn't win people to Christ.

Instead we're called to love our neighbor, and part of that is showing them what God's love can do.

When you are overcome with love, wear it. Say it. Claim it. Profess it. Don't keep quiet because you're afraid. And most of all, feel it. Feel the feelings of joy and gratitude, and tell of his perfection. When it makes sense, when it matches, when it is right, you know it. Sometimes that means challenging a misbelief, and sometimes that means keeping quiet. Wisdom is just one of our gifts as God's beloved.

Take the socks off the rooster. They are of no use. Not one of us was meant for the itchy stress of trying to fit in. We were created for the freedom of peace. Run through the barnyard footloose and fancy-free, leave the socks in the henhouse, and paint your roof red with your testimony!

Today look for a chance to share your thanksgiving for what God has done for you lately.

THE FINISHING TOUCH

Lord God, you created me for the freedom of peace. You are mighty to save, one with who I am because of you who is without beginning or end. I am never neglected or unheard. I will shout your goodness from the rooftops. It is well. Amen.

DAY 14

The Top Out

*Today I have given you the choice between life
and death, between blessings and curses.
Now I call on heaven and earth to witness the choice
you make. Oh, that you would choose life, so
that you and your descendants might live!*

DEUTERONOMY 30:19 NLT

Not much can be done on the interior of a house until it has a roof. Then a plumber is invited to pipe out sinks, showers, and toilets. But the most important part of the plumbing top out is ventilating the plumbing stacks. Why would we want to cut holes in that perfect roof to vent the plumbing? It's water, not air.

Sewage stinks.

Frankly, I'd rather not talk about it. I want our heart renovations to be fun. I want to talk about paint colors and bold rose-colored floral prints. But the fact is, if your heart-head plumbing isn't vented, water won't flow through the pipes. And then, my friend, you have sewage in your sink.

Being stagnant stinks. And it sure wasn't what I expected when I asked Jesus to be the

Lord of renovating my life and cleaning out the mess. Saved means free. Saved means loved, protected, and secure.

But then I'm here with all the smelly stress. Can you identify?

My guess is that when our heart-head is full of sewage it's because we looked at what God was asking us to do (release control of when we might get married, wait patiently for that new job, give away most of that bonus check, stop worrying about what our old church thinks of us, or be kind to that brat occupying the desk next to us) and slapped a big N-O on God's scary-looking plan. Who needs a gaping hole in the plans for their life?

Clinging to your expectations and plans, negative thinking, worst-case-scenario dreaming, and limited believing is what's plugging up your pipes.

Oh my goodness, this God, whose ways are perfect and who knows the plans he has for us, is capable of providing mountain-moving, water-walking, dead-to-alive, miraculous living. Yet we box him in to our meager understanding and fight the wisdom of having a hole in our roof—and slap a big old pipe cap on the flow of his goodness, hope, joy, mystery, and glory.

Here's the thing. You have access to the fullness of God's power and can simultaneously experience how he flows when you ask for it. I know you think you know what God is capable of. But are you living like you know? I am inviting you to the practice of really knowing, really feeling that God is going to come through. This requires doing scary things.

Cutting holes in a new roof—releasing whatever we consider our protection and instead expecting God to fulfill his promises—is uncomfortable and maybe even painful. Letting go of the control of what comes *into* our life is scary. What if it rains? What if God makes me be single forever? What if I lose my job? What if . . . ugh . . .

But do you want to flush out the stress? Okay, then there has to be space for the fresh wind of God to enter your heart-head so the sewage can escape. I know it doesn't feel like positive change, but that's the subconscious clinging to what's comfortable, not what's best.

It's wishful thinking to believe that we can confine the power of God. However, remember, he is a gentleman who gave us free will. And while he will never leave or forsake us, his power won't flow easily when we slap our will over him and dictate his character, will, or being. And this is where I must tell you, you have to blow your stack.

Let it out. Talk to (or yell at) God. Say all the things out loud while looking in a mirror so it is a visual and auditory experience for the heart-head, or write it all out. Feel and then let go of disappointment, worry, and unrest. If you are writing it, sign your full name at the bottom, like you are signing something important. This is a controlled, intentional way to blow your stack.

Now . . .

Let Jesus be Jesus. Expect him to function and flow, and then choose to feel passion, delight, and wonder. That is how it works, and I think you'll be quite pleased with the results.

THE FINISHING TOUCH

Thank you, Jesus, for being you. Thank you for your ease. I am willing to open my hands, vent the pipes, and watch you flow in and push the sewage out! Amen.

Mind Makeover

We've explored the process of purposefully allowing in new beliefs. This is a significant step to recognize and blow out our old, established beliefs that limit us and lead to worry and stress.

- *Make a running list of things that pop into your mind that you recognize as limited or unhelpful beliefs.*

Function and style aside, we have a culture that is quick to tell us who Jesus is and how he moves. But as we recognize the fact that my style is not yours and my experiences are different from what you have experienced, we also recognize that Christ meets us individually and uniquely.

- *How do you meet with him? What does he sound like? How do you feel when he is flowing through you and not being held tight within the confines of what you think is possible?*

Use one of the statements below as a breath prayer for the next few days as you allow him to step into your life and fulfill his promises to you.

Jesus is working in my life.

Jesus always finishes what he starts.

My passion for Jesus is without measure.

Jesus flows continuously in my life.

DAY 16

Chairs, Me, and Jesus

Give all your worries and cares to God,
for he cares about you.

1 Peter 5:7 nlt

I have probably reupholstered ninety-nine chairs in my lifetime. My chair thing started when I was a young mother of two, with number three on the way, and I volunteered with a local women's club.

If I am honest, I joined for the points. You know, brownie points with God. But really, I was interested in getting out of the house and being around adult humans. Can I get an amen?

One night while working at a silent auction for the club, the most beautiful occasional chair I had ever seen was put on the auction block. The French provincial side chair was decorated with intricately carved mahogany and gold-and-white-striped fabric. On each of the white stripes was a repeating pattern of blue, gold, and scarlet roses and delicate hunter-green leaves.

It was exquisite—way fancier than the other chairs I owned, most likely more expensive than all my furniture investments combined. And I wanted that chair. Lucky for

me, I was working behind the scenes and could monitor the chair, and I opened with a bid of fifty dollars. It never went any higher. I won by default.

But it was when I hauled my fifty-dollar find home that the real delight came. On the underside of the chair was a tag that read, "Custom Order for Jami McKelvey 9/26/85. $1700.00." The significance of this is outstanding. First, a $1,700 chair? For $50? Second, Jami—no "e." Third, McKelvie is my maiden name. Granted, it was spelled differently on the tag, but come on? And finally, my birthday is September 26. That chair had been in a furniture warehouse with my name and birthday on it for nearly fifteen years.

In previous days we discussed our expectations along with the color red. Now I want us to think of the color red as warnings signs, where we stop and acknowledge the truths that we have forgotten.

One of those truths is this: we are never unseen.

And if you feel like you've been abandoned, these words are a red stop sign.

Stop.

Now.

Of course, we aren't stopping because an eighteen-wheeler is about to plow into us—we are stopping to give thanks because we are seen, heard, and known.

I hear from so many readers: "I feel like God never answers me." And I understand this.

But God's timing and provision aren't like a genie in a bottle. If you're at all like me, while praying for little things like finding my missing glove or making it to the school in time to pick up my kid despite the fact that I left late, I end up repeating the words "I feel like he never answers me," and it teaches my heart-head that God isn't who he says he is. And then when the big stuff comes, I'm spring-loaded to remember the times I felt unseen rather than all those times God had the perfect chair sitting in a warehouse for me.

Instead let's practice seeing when God shows up so we can expect God to show up—and then we can say thank you, which only adds feel-good feelings to the whole kit and caboodle. These positive practices teach the heart-head the truth of who God is in a way that it can *learn*. Remember, the heart-head tends to remember what is most rehearsed.

Today sit in your comfiest of chairs and recall two times you felt seen by God and then have a private (or not-so-private) party. Write down what happened (or maybe even draw a picture). Post the notes where you'll see them every day. Then you might have a square of chocolate or buy yourself some flowers, or you can do like the ancient Israelites did in Joshua 4: grab a stone and set it up as a reminder that God sees us and shows up. When we rehearse good things, our body releases the hormones of peace and joy.[4] It's a great lesson to be learned seated comfortably at the feet of he who rather likes you.

THE FINISHING TOUCH

Jesus, I love you. I love that you know me and know what I love.
I can rest well knowing that you are always with me.
Thank you. Amen.

DAY 17

In the Kitchen with Martha

"Martha, Martha," the Lord answered, "you are worried and upset about many things, but few things are needed—or indeed only one."

LUKE 10:41–42

Martha is my favorite biblical heroine. But she only became so after I read Katie M. Reid's book *Made like Martha: Good News for the Woman Who Gets Things Done* and realized something important.

Jesus wasn't chastising Martha. He was inviting her to rest. For the years prior to falling headlong into the welcoming arms of grace, I believed Martha to be a bad girl like me. Unable to be more like quiet Mary, I cursed the type A Martha in me and hung the faux tapestry of religious rituals, desperately hoping to *look* better even if I couldn't *feel* better.

I attended workshops and retreats all with the singular goal of forcing Martha to the feet of Jesus. The years of condemnation and shame that followed only created more rebellion and strife simply because I believed God had knit me together wrong.

My poor "old self" was listening to the lies of stuffy religion rather than the truth of God, and let me tell you . . . that never goes well. When we fight against God's intentional design, the flow is interrupted.

In kitchen renovation, the most common complaint is about the flow of the design. A U-shaped kitchen allows the homeowner to work in an arc. A galley kitchen might require the owner to turn back and forth from the sink to the stove. And an L-shaped kitchen usually offers a more open feel that allows whoever is in the kitchen to still be a part of the conversation. But if your sink is next to the fridge and the stove is in the pantry, your flow is a lot more work than your twenty-minute dumplings can comprehend.

When I thought I was in trouble for my natural "can do!" and "get it done!" design, I was stressed and worried, believing I was in trouble for the *wrong kind* of trying. Then I *tried* to rest. But then I wondered, who was going to plan parties, iron doilies, and refinish that antique buffet I bought from Craigslist? Still me—only I was tackily decorated in "should" and "shouldn't" and "I'm sick to death of myself and my Marthaesque ways."

Martha was in the kitchen because she was the hostess with the mostest. Teresa of Ávila (who was kind of a superstar believer in the 1500s) said, "Love turns work into rest."[5] When we approach anything, even our quiet time in the morning, as hard or "have to," it is no longer enjoyable or restful—we've put our stove in the garage. There's absolutely no flow there. When we cease to strive, when we are motivated and enriched by that which we were created for, it might look like Mary's chill vibe, but it is simply work we love.

In the freedom of grace, in the comfiness of unconditional love, I can embrace my God-given Martha talents and abilities and simultaneously be as mellow as Mary, sipping lattes and smelling the roses.

Are you a Mary, wishing you could be more like Martha? (Although you might also be thinking, *Ugh, I hate to be bossy—alas, Marthas roll how they roll.*) Your Mary qualities may have led to your being falsely accused of laziness, just some flim-flam decor that never seems to finish anything she starts.

But that's not true. God doesn't make mistakes. Thank goodness you don't have to worry about that!

So which are you? Mary or Martha? List out five *good* things about your natural personality. Now write out how God might use those good traits, and be on the lookout to employ them today.

THE FINISHING TOUCH

Lord God, thank you for my unique creation. Thank you that I no longer have to struggle and strive to be different than you intended. I am so grateful that I am created for the balance of work and the refuge of rest. Amen.

DAY 18

Stop on Red

*Pay attention to what I say; turn
your ear to my words.*

PROVERBS 4:20

I love red. My kitchen is a rusty-rose red. And I have a habit of using matte red lipstick and wearing floral-printed red maxi dresses and blouses. Second only to my obsession with cobalt blue is my consistent desire to decorate and express myself in shades of red.

However, I had not ever really considered the *feelings* of red until we moved to Houston.

The home we purchased has a quirky yet endearing foyer. It is too big to just be a foyer and too small to be anything else. When we bought it, we discovered that the previous owners had set it up as a reading nook, painted a rich, red-hot scarlet.

As much as I love red, the entry room felt very *hot.*

Let me pause here to say that I am a professional artist with art in major national retailers. This credential doesn't transfer to wall paint. And I am a professional teacher and life coach. Those credentials neither trans-fer to nor help in my ability to wrap gifts, effectively use Scotch tape, or paint walls. After an incident in 1996 involving a gallon of Sunset Poppy Satin

Finish and no drop cloth, in an effort to save my marriage, I agreed never to roll any color on any dwelling until *ever again.*

One day, while Justin was out of town, the foyer burned my retinas so badly that I couldn't stand it anymore.

So, I bought a can of Bluebonnet Skies and made a mockery out of the painter's trade. I arranged furniture and a rug, hung pictures, and changed the curtains. Still, there was no hiding my betrayal. Lucky for me, we enter our home through the garage. So it was two weeks before Justin even noticed the debacle I called, "Finished . . . kind of." My defense of third-degree retina burn didn't change the fact that I'd broken a promise. Of course, my sweet husband forgave me, and we were able to put our marriage back together. The room? Well, we just don't go in that room. We will deal with it when we move.

But this mess is like the mess most of us are in: cleaning up after ourselves when our reactions take us places we really have no business being.

Red-hot, nonsensical reactions are not part of a life in Christ. However, we must live in bodies that may or not own a pair of blood-red pleather pants bought on impulse. (Not me, I don't have the emotional endurance for pleather. I actually made that choice rationally.) The animal part of the brain is the reactive part that gets you to run from an aggressive dog at the park or pull your hand quickly from something hot.

When I say "animal brain," what do you think of? To stop—which in our culture we recognize as a red octagon—and think about what you are thinking allows a worried or stressed mind to organize thoughts rationally.

Lucky for you, you have the mind of Christ . . . when you stop and remind yourself through sensory effort.

I made a poor decision when I decided to paint whatever that entry room is. But had I stopped and thought about what I was thinking, why I was reacting the way I was reacting, what better outcome could there have been? I likely wouldn't have responded with what Justin would call an irrational decision. I wouldn't have spiraled into a mind game of *I didn't*

honor my husband . . . I disappointed God. And there wouldn't have been the tedious physical hurdles of trying to keep Justin from using the front door *ever again.*

When we stop and consider how we are responding, activating our breath and quality questions that engage all the brain, we experience the tangible feelings of peace.

Is there any part of your brain that thinks what I am suggesting is "not faith"? See, we have memorized Scriptures and recited practices that have confused our signals and possibly led us to believe that thinking and faith are mutually exclusive. This is the opportunity to *stop*, know your thoughts, and then organize them in a tangible-feeling way to teach the mind what you want it to recognize as unshakable faith.

So say you spill bright-red paint on the carpet and then pray to Jesus that your husband never, ever, ever moves that ottoman. What does the heart-head have to resolve? Well, it has something to hide. And it doesn't want to be in trouble. But what does the Bible say about confession? Honesty? Honoring my husband? Okay . . . wait, am I activating the animal brain with its hot-button decisions? Or am I activating the mind of Christ?

Love and fear cannot be mixed—they don't compute. Acknowledging this—understanding that our focus is on Christ, not the law or church regulations or habitual practices—allows us to learn to know him through our own experiences. This space of clarity, where I stop and check in before I check out with another gallon of paint, is the place where the Holy Spirit can wash us and remind us of the truths about ourselves in Christ.

We make mistakes or react inappropriately, and the heart-head has more problems to solve. Stopping to evaluate teaches the mind to believe what we are saying.

Think about this: Why does a rowdy rendition of "I Surrender All" during worship feel so good? Music is a sensory experience that raises our emotions (energy in the body). That feel-good energy tells the subconscious something—"That feels so right and good!" On the flip side, if your music pastor is out with the flu and the "good servant" who volunteered to fill in sounds like a strangled cat, the church's AC is out, and the crotch of your pantyhose is at your knees and causing unreasonable chaffing, animal brain doesn't like Jesus.

I have grown in my walk with him through Bible study and worship. However, when that feel-good, Jesus-loves-me emotion crashes against anger and destruction, and I focus entirely on a God who destroys and sends plagues and swarms of crunchy bugs, I end up one stressed lady. Without context and an understanding about what we really believe, these terrifying images of God leave the heart-head soaked in paint, with tennis shoes ruined, baseboards stained, and in trouble with only ourselves. Nothing can separate you from the love of God except for you believing that you are separated.

Sis, you gotta feel it if you want it to compute. I don't want to boss you, but you have to know what's going on behind that wall before you paint it a different color. What are your feelings teaching you? One bad day at church might not impact you. Twenty Sundays in a row of something that makes you miserable and broken? You are teaching the heart-head something.

Organize your mind by listening to what you are actually thinking, beloved. Write your thoughts out, write them in red, and ask this God who adores you to lead you to feel and react in ways that delight him and lead you into his peace. Stop. Do it right now.

THE FINISHING TOUCH

Jesus, stop me with your whisper. Ground me in your tangible and undeniable presence. Wisdom is mine when I listen to you and practice the feelings of your eternal and precious love. Amen.

DAY 19

Feel of It

Therefore, since we are receiving a kingdom that
cannot be shaken, let us be thankful, and so worship
God acceptably with reverence and awe.

HEBREWS 12:28

My husband, Justin, and I have spent 75 percent of our marriage in a West Texas town. Although we haven't always lived there, certain regional phrases have made their way into our vocabulary. I don't know what to use in place of "y'all," and I have been known to say "fixin' to" and "Mister, you get your boots on and get on back up to the house!"

At least we've learned to steer clear of "I'll tell you what" and "I have an idear."

Bless our little hearts. Still another Texas slang phrase that we forgo slinging is "feel of it."

Feel of it, as in "touch this."

But I'm going to break my linguistic guidelines and invite you to *feel of it*—and I mean get in there and get a good feel of God.

Over the next few days, I am going to say some pretty bold things about our Creator, and I pray you *feel* them. Not because of my mad writing skills or my obsession with all things DIY (do it yourself) and DIA (do it again), but because when you feel the difference between worry and peace and between strife and joy, your mind will note the difference and change.

God invited us to a stress-free existence when we first said, "Yes, Lord!" However, not long after we slipped into the comforts of our newly designed peaceful existence, someone or something—society, church, or just staying steeped in law-bound practice—lined our heart-heads with the world's most pokey cacti. All of which makes us wonder what went wrong with God's plan.

There is no lack in God's plan for your freedom. Worry and stress are interferences in his will for your life.

I propose that the previous statement caused you stress. Why? Because it means you've brought on your own stress. You have taken on salvation, your yes to Jesus and his promises, as a *burden*. You're trying to pay Jesus back for his work on the cross. And you decided you *should* be this way or that way.

Friend, you weren't designed to have to earn Jesus's love. A good design doesn't have to try to be a good design—it just is.

As we're getting a good feel of God, let me stop here and say that while I'm the scribe of these tales and textures, I'm on a journey too. And sometimes I don't know what I am stressed or doubtful about until I stop and assess those feelings.

When I first started my renovation, I had a heart-head full of uncomfortable religious obligation and misunderstandings. I bet you suspect you have some misunderstandings, too, but I cannot *know* them for you. You have to discover them for yourself.

Let's all remember the importance of thinking and discerning as we sit in our recliners, mindlessly scrolling at the speed of 5G. We're inundated with other people's issues, opinions, rants, raves, and trials. We are constantly feeling of it. But the feelings we are not cognizant of, the images and arguments of strife and ugliness, play out in our minds as if they were really happening to us, right there in our La-Z-Boys.

Jesus asks us to be still and *know* who he is. Knowing the truth of Jesus, discerning the rock-solid truth gives us an aesthetic break from overstimulation and stress. But we can't know until we know. You know?

We need to dig in to his words so we can get a real feel of him and be able to recognize his quiet invitation, which will allow our minds a place to declutter, reboot, and rest.

Today, I would like to suggest you "feel of it." This is a practice in paying attention to what you've been missing. I recommend having a little notebook and pen handy. Today if you catch yourself laughing out loud or a lump rising in your throat, *stop*! What caused that reaction? Write about it. Start a list of things you feel.

THE FINISHING TOUCH

Jesus, open my eyes. Let me see, hear, and feel you near. Let me wander the halls of my peaceful heart-head, not in search of you but led by you. Amen.

Mind Makeover

We've focused on our relationship with the authentic Jesus—getting seated and centering our attention wholly on him.

- *Are you noticing the feelings of belief and freedom versus strife and stress?*

- *What are the feelings? Describe what you feel and where in your body. For example, my left knee twitches when I am excited. When I laugh, I feel relief in my shoulders. Certain songs make my torso feel twitchy. Taking note of these feelings is communicating your physical, emotional, and spiritual design.*

Whether the color red makes you feel hot and bothered or as footloose and fancy-free as a girl in a red convertible, believers have an association with red. The letters in red in our Bibles give us actual words spoken by Jesus. Red blood signifies God's grace, forgiveness, and sacrifice. What does red make you feel? Take some time to spy red in nature. Be cognizant of red, and then stop and notice the feelings you have. Please pick one of the statements below to use in reference to red and the pure white lamb, whose sacrifice assures our wholeness.

🌸 Lord, speak to me—I'm listening.

🌸 Let Jesus be Jesus.

🌸 I am a creation of thought and feeling.

🌸 I give thanks from the depths of my heart for all things.

SECTION THREE
Neutrally Yours

DAY 21

White As...

*His appearance was like lightning,
and his clothes were white as snow.*

MATTHEW 28:3

Joanna Gaines of the popular HGTV hit *Fixer Upper* made white and neutral color palettes and her farmhouse industrial style fashionable trends. And now white is all up in my eclectic business. I mean, Joanna's style with the rustic white walls, exposed beams, brick, and weathering is all the rage for a reason. It is pretty cool to see old made new.

But I gotta have a lot more color than white—and not just because I have six kids. I love color. Big, bold mismatched colors and wild floral posies are my favorite.

But I also recognize I would have none of this without white.

How's that?

White is used to lighten a darker color. It is also used to accent or highlight a color or pattern. And a white front door, as you might suspect, is indicative of a residence that is clean and well organized. Currently my front door is red . . . just come through the garage.

Recently while binge-watching some DIY program, I was mesmerized by a home—I mean, it was someone's home, but it was actually a twenty-four-thousand-square-foot mansion. Everything in this estate was white. Floors, decor, even the Bentley in the garage. And all of it was kept glossy, bleached, and polished by a full staff . . . that the owners of all that white can pay because they're wealthy.

Come to think of it, white plays into how we label work. Blue collar gets dirty. White collar stays clean.

But the color white is neutral. And this is the big role that white plays in this section. We need to get neutral about some of the things we are programmed by culture to take at face value. We'll call this neutral zone white space.

In art and design, white space is any area not taken up by a subject.

In this case, I am here to usher in a heart-head space that is stress-free. But there's no room in your mind when it is buzzing with looming what-ifs or when you're *thinking*—trying to solve, list, or remember—or *creating*, as in imag-ining a scenario. Many times these processes can turn into a downward spiral and make you feel more anxious. But when you *realize* you are thinking or creating, you're open to *receiving* good things.

And this is my neutral proposal to you. It's a useful technique in any worrisome mind space.

Stop.

Close your eyes and picture white light. Breathe in and out slowly to the count of ten, and then, in your mind, ask yourself this question: "Am I thinking, creating, or receiving?"

Keep your eyes closed and focus on the white until you feel calm white space. Don't judge yourself for your response. Just neutrally no-tice—thinking, creating, or receiving.

Very often when we practice neutrality, we will more clearly rec-ognize we are not in real danger, don't need to stress, and can release our fears. From this objective space we can see and receive solutions to our worries and finally experience earth as it is in heaven.

God wants to give you peace. There is no mixed message in love. Love without contingency does not require tending it in order to keep it. Again and again I will say there is no *but* in a perfect "I love you." "I love you, but . . ." has a shade added to it. It requires the recipient to behave a certain way.

God just loves you. Period.

Picture the pure white light of God's love. Let go of your fears. Ask him to come into your heart-head. Now visualize his light flooding through you. It enters through your head, washing away the concerns, leaving behind a light, free place.

Ahhhh. Clean white walls.

THE FINISHING TOUCH

Jesus, be with me as I ask, "Am I thinking, creating, or receiving?"
Open my mind. Clean the walls of my heart-head to white
as white can be. Amen.

DAY 22

Hard Hat Area

*Put on the full
armor of God.*

Ephesians 6:11

In our family shop, we have all kinds of hard hats. Our sons Sam and Charlie like to wear them when they play. Granted, they have been known to do this barefoot, and on a couple of occasions, in their underwear . . . outside. The neighbors love us.

In real construction, most sites require hard hats to protect workers and visitors from ending up with busted craniums. I think we'd all agree that wearing a hard hat to a building in process is a good idea. But having equipment to keep us safe is only helpful when we use that equipment properly.

While the brain (that physical thing in your skull) is soft and spongy, the mind (the mental part of you that processes information) is as hard as . . . well, a hard hat. The mind wants to be set in its ways and is slow to change its beliefs, habits, or convictions.

While we wait for change, our minds say, "In the meantime, I'll slap on the hard hat of protection and just keep watching for and protecting us against the bad stuff coming." Worse, without the physical feelings of proven change, the heart-head constantly recounts the past and becomes a faith bulldozer wholly doubting and demolishing the bright future we were promised.

Trust me. I am experiencing this as I write. We are hunting for a different house, with a set budget and precise location. It's not going well. And I could vent my frustrations, but that won't help. Whatever happens may not be exactly what I am expecting, but my protection, advancement, and success are promised.

The only option for penetrating our mind's stubborn ways is to give it new experiences. Experiences that are more appealing and *feel* better than the thoughts the heart-head is harboring and practicing on repeat.

Time to suit up and actually do something to protect that fretful mind. The Holy Spirit said our minds could be transformed (Romans 12:2). And I believe him.

We started the process of excising stress yesterday by stopping and giving the mind time to tune in to thoughts and feelings. By taking a moment and processing whether we're thinking (how to solve our problems) and creating (what might happen), we are actively taking our thoughts captive so we can receive (take in the good things). This is different from the thinking and creating of spiraling thoughts and creating of worst-case scenarios.

When we take these measures in conjunction with deep breaths, we stabilize the body and cease the release of stress hormones. We are inviting God to protect us.

When we invoke the question, "Am I thinking, creating, or receiving?" the brain stops to analyze, and we aren't panicking anymore. Like a child counting down the days to summer vacation or Christmas morning, we can wait with joyful expectation for an answer to all our woes, while simultaneously creating feel-good feelings, triggering the body to produce more dopamine (a feel-good hormone) instead of more cortisol and adrenaline (the stress hormones).

When we give thanks and feel the feelings of appreciation and gratitude, we invite Jesus into the situation, choose to trust his protection, and voice our desire to receive the good things he has for us. We say thank you for the roof currently over my head, for the resources we have, for what we know God will do to care for us.

Feeling these feelings of appreciation retrains our minds and bodies and completely renovates our spiritual journeys. We are then able to move from fretful, worrisome thoughts to peace-filled, divinely directed learning to love.

I want you to do something tangible. Even if it feels silly, you are the teacher, and your mind is the student.

Write out a scriptural promise you want to live. Pin it to your blouse or write it on your palm, but actually put it on your person. Every time you notice it say, "I am covered by Jesus!" Feel it, celebrate it, and choose to be covered. Soon you'll be saying, "Wow. That's crazy amazing!" and "Lord, I know you'll show up."

You brave thing!

THE FINISHING TOUCH

I am dressed and ready for the change from stress and strife to peace and praise. I love you, and I thank you. I am so thankful that you have me covered. Amen.

DAY 23

Curb Appeal

*And the peace of God that surpasses all
understanding will guard your
hearts and minds in Christ Jesus.*

PHILIPPIANS 4:7 NET

C urb appeal is the charm of a home from the street view. However, curb appeal is not just about cleverly hung ferns, pops of colorful bulb flowers, and trained vines that climb perfectly from the garden bed to the gingerbread eaves. If your door is professionally painted a lovely shade of sage, your gutters are clean, and your garage door is a flawless match, but your address intersects with Busiest Street in Town Boulevard, your curb appeal is toast.

On the other side of curb appeal is the appeal of expecting to feel at home. Most homeowners know the value of a cul-de-sac or at least a few feet of privacy and quiet. As someone who craves outdoor space, quiet, and no street noise, I have great compassion for families living about nine miles from our current home. A new highway, one that connects the bustling university town of College Station to the big city of Houston, is under construction. Homes that once faced

soaring forests, burn-your-eyes blue skies, and open fields of grazing wild-life now get the not-so-stunning view of a toll road.

When the owners of those homes originally planted their dreams, they probably weren't expecting their front yard would become an eight-lane highway. The FOR SALE signs that now decorate their yards indicate they don't expect to be satisfied there any longer and hope to relocate before the first toll is collected.

But I wonder, who would want to purchase a home with a compromised and permanent lack of curb appeal?

Someone will. Some humans don't care so much about highway noise and pollution.

This is where we will delve into the practice of neutrality. When we scroll on our phones or watch 24-7 news networks, we are in a constant mind space of judgment. However, now that we've identified the problem, we have the opportunity to grab and knock it into . . . the great white.

Let's pretend you are watching the news, unwinding after a long day at the office. Suddenly a story about the highway I just mentioned comes on. An elderly widow is crying into the camera about her home of sixty-six years being run over by the construction of the highway. You feel sad for her. And then the legislator responsible for getting the toll road approved comes on and says, "The old woman needs to move to a retirement home and stop whining!" Now you feel enraged. Cue the adrenaline.

You may still be seated in your comfy, safe home, but your brain is taking on Congress and the Department of Transportation. But let me ask you, are you in a position to do anything about this situation? If you are, go do it. You are primed and hopped up on cortisol. Storm the castle, shoog.

But if you are not, if there is nothing to be done physically or financially, your most powerful help is to close your eyes, take ten deep breaths, and ask, "Am I thinking, creating, or receiving?" Wait a few moments, and then, in your mind, paint the news report white. Yes, you can pray for that woman—heck, pray for that meathead of a politician who put a toll booth in her rose garden—and *then go neutral.*

You have real-life things to tend to. Save your adrenaline for a high-speed chase of your toddler around the living room. You can receive the appealing peace right there on your curb. You change the narrative.

So if you think about your dearly departed mother, you may be moved to tears, but you can consciously say to yourself, "At least she is in heaven now."

And of course you miss her. But you are different now that she is with Jesus, and we want to teach our heart-head that we really do believe in eternal life, peace, and joy. We do that by switching the narrative to the feel-good part of "She is in heaven with Jesus for the love. She is having the time of her eternal life." Write your emotions about an event or loss, then flip the narrative to a story with all the appeal of a Sunday drive on a quiet, wooded country road. Nice!

THE FINISHING TOUCH

No matter where I am, no matter what intrusions I face, you, Lord Jesus, are my comfort and strength. I choose to actively remain in your calm presence. Amen.

White Walls

*I can do all things through him
who strengthens me.*

PHILIPPIANS 4:13 ESV

W e finally get to play with the good stuff. Remember, your foundation is solid (God), your heart-head home has good bones, the plumbing is topped out, and the roof, windows, and doors are secure. Which brings us to the white part of the process—Sheetrock, tape, bed, and texture.

How much do you wish you could re-rock your heart-head and get the white space you need to calm your mind, turn off the stress hounds, and be the clear-thinking, divine creation your loving God created you to be?

Since my family's home is for sale, Justin is staying at our empty house to manage the showings. Sam, Charlie, and I are living with my mom and dad. I was legitimately surprised when a month passed and the house had not sold. So I got comfy and still, and I said out loud, "Jesus, I need to *not* live with my parents. Please sell my house." Then I closed my eyes, inhaled and exhaled, and then whispered, "Am I thinking, creating, or receiving?" Thinking was a mess of ideas. But then creating and receiving began!

Immediately, a blank canvas

flashed in my mind. I intentionally imagined myself writing "I can do all things through Christ" in huge cobalt blue letters. I wrote it again and again and I received the feelings of this truth.

And that is when I was interrupted by the thought: *The house can't sell—you haven't left yet.*

At first this frustrated me. There is no furniture in the house. I live with my mother. I moved out. But I forced myself back to, "Am I thinking, creating, or receiving?" And . . .

I hadn't left emotionally yet.

When Justin and I ate lunch or went to meet our real estate agent, we only talked about why we thought the house hadn't sold.

And I realized, I believed all those things that were wrong would prevent God from being big enough to sell my house. So I went to the house to say goodbye.

Before you call me a hippie dip, hear me out. I went to the house. I rang the doorbell, and I walked through the house and . . . talked to it. If your "she's weird" alarm bells went off right now, I get it. However, I quickly realized I was still attached to the house.

Yes, I moved out, but I had not had a closing to the thought, *I am moving.* Think about funerals and New Year's Eve parties. We mark the ends of events with actions. Those actions imprint the heart-head with feelings that allow it to move on.

In that house I'd launched two of my six children, written two books, homeschooled my kids, and met with suffering and triumph. The feelings I had in that house taught me something. And now it only makes sense that I needed to have a ceremony of sorts to close the chapter.

From there I chose to receive whatever God had for me.

The receiving was nothing short of miraculous.

My house sold four days after I said goodbye. Above asking price, full cash, two weeks close. The new owners? A woman, her husband, and their six homeschooled children (the same as my family). Oh! And the woman just wrote her first book.

We are promised miracles. If you're wondering why you don't see miracles, it's because we cannot spy them until the walls of our heart-heads are primed and ready. Our brains see and experience what we are used to.

What are you missing? Where do you need to see God? Are you still supposed to be at that house, job, school, relationship? Are you open to seeing a miracle, even if it isn't where you expect to see it?

Today ask yourself, "What wall needs to be stripped down to the studs? What physical act can I do to help my heart-head feel the conclusion so I can move on to the next solution?" Burning a letter, dunking yourself in the bathtub, or going outside and screaming all signify something to the mind—"That is done. Let's move on." Then receive the goodness God has in whatever circumstance you're in.

If those walls could talk, they could tell some stories.

THE FINISHING TOUCH

Jesus, thank you for always coming through. Thank you for the newness all around me. I believe you. I trust you. I love being invited to share my life with you and experience all the wonders of real belief. No worries. Amen.

Mind Makeover

We've added a new tool to our pouch. The white-light visualization and questioning of our trains of thought are going to advance us greatly. The mind operates from experience. By challenging past experiences and inviting the heart-head to catch up with the conscious mind, we are able to identify worrisome triggers. Furthermore, we participate in the prayers we profess by attaching feel-good, oxygenated feelings to the process. The heart-head is energized by choosing to leave behind dark worry and will be more cooperative as you progress in your renovation. Say the key question to yourself often: Am I thinking, creating, or receiving?

I encourage you to write down your experiences so you can go back and revisit the miracles you've found. For example, my journal pages have dog-ears and Post-its marking answers to prayer. We might acknowledge verbally, "Oh wow! Thank you, God!" But when we mark an occasion physically, with pen and paper, and feel the feelings of a tangible God? The heart-head pays attention!

DAY 26

Plenty of Seats

Do not worry about tomorrow, for tomorrow will worry about itself. Each day has enough trouble of its own.

MATTHEW 6:34

The latest chairs Jesus gifted me came in a set of three. They are comfy and cozy, and they were free. The only issue was convincing Justin to haul them to our home. He was less than enthused. And not just because they are white . . . and we live with Sam and Charlie . . . but because Justin finds it eerie that odd occasional chairs hunt me down and demand to take a place in our home.

Every bit of extra furniture I hear about, I respond, "I'll take it."

I don't know what for, but I'm addicted to the hidden messages in every piece I encounter. I mean, look at me now. Writing and illustrating a book about all the ways I've met with Jesus

in the process of re-covering, rearranging, and giving fresh eyes to a project.

So with some sweet talk from me and a secondary mission to pick up Thai food, Justin picked up the chairs. I could hardly wait for them to arrive. Until they did, and then I thought, *I don't know why we need these huge chairs.* Sam and Charlie were forbidden from getting within three feet of the high-end mini sofas. In fact, I bribed them with cookies not to look directly at the chairs, so as not to be lured into the fluffy comfort of their stark white arms.

Our family room is directly above the garage and is the same size—two cars wide. It was already furnished with three large sofas, a recliner, and a game table next to a kitchenette. But I knew the three white chairs needed to be added to the seating options. Well, for anyone thirty-two and older, with clean hands!

So after three frustrating hours of trying to make the room and chairs work, I sat on the floor, closed my eyes, and started to deep breathe, picturing God's white light washing through me. When the stress dissolved, I asked myself, "Jami, are you thinking, creating, or receiving?" I definitely wasn't receiving. My mind was thinking through all the alternatives and creating disastrous scenarios (including throwing out every stick of furniture in the room).

And in a flash, I saw the room as it could be.

I confess—the big white chairs were rarely sat upon, even by approved sitters. Until Christmas 2021, when twenty-four family members gathered in our home to celebrate. And in my family room over the garage, a feeling of contentment washed over me.

Everyone was comfortably seated.

We borrow a lot of trouble from tomorrow, when right now, in this second, it's okay. You are okay. Perhaps this is bold of me to say. However, you are reading a pretty good little book. Do you like the pictures? Me too.

Knowing you have been looked after is darling. It's a great comfort to discover what you need was always right in front of you. In my case, with the big white chairs, I had an opportunity to speak truth to my heart-head so it could learn something new. As I review what happened even now, I assign the good feelings to the God who knows me. I imagine his white light flooding through me, washing away the dark stress. I've learned to believe as I receive. Not things. Not the chairs. (This is not about wishing things into existence!)

Get seated, get still, and imagine the white light of God flowing through you. Experience the true character of Jesus. Pure love is moving all around us. Jesus will bring earth as it is in heaven. That promise isn't some flimsy fabric treatment to protect us. It is the truth of what he came to set us free from. Worry and strife are the stain. Jesus is the solvent.

Be at rest in this. Be activating your mind through questions. Think through a recent time when you were worried or stressed. Were you thinking? Creating? Were you borrowing trouble from the future or the past? Now process through what it would look like to anticipate receiving from a loving, all-powerful God. Sit in the throne of peace and wisdom, which he picked just for you.

THE FINISHING TOUCH

Jesus, I choose to take my thoughts captive, question more, create from a space of clarity, and receive from the confident seat of your friendship. Amen.

DAY 27

In the Mix

For I am convinced that neither death nor life, neither angels nor demons, neither the present nor the future, nor any powers, neither height nor depth, nor anything else in all creation, will be able to separate us from the love of God that is in Christ Jesus our Lord.

ROMANS 8:38–39

Monochromatic, the use of one color in varying depths and shades, is not my jam. I love assembling splashes of color, and I will absolutely mix patterns.

I adore changing colors in a space and experimenting with blends of color and pattern. But when it comes to paint, you get what you mix.

If you pour white paint into a can of Smoky Night Navy and give it a vigorous shake, those mix and form a lighter shade of blue. Once this happens, there's no way you can separate the two paints. They are *of* each other and are something entirely different and new.

Shoog, that is an image of you and God. When you allow God to pour into you, he can't be separated out again. It's impossible to separate you from the God who loves you.

To help you stimulate even more good changes in how you think, grab a pen and paper and write out what God is currently gifting you and how you plan to *receive* all that goodness. As you hold that pen in your hand, know that Jesus is right there in the mix, cheering you on, absolutely determined to work all things out for your good.

By physically writing the words, we invite our heart-head into the process of solidifying what's real. Even more, using pen and paper helps you *feel* a connection between the words in your head and the disturbances in your heart. This stimulates and activates all the happy functions of the brain. White paper with room to doodle, script, print, and color sends a message to the brain: "Hey, she is serious about this—look at the details." When faced with a worry or struggle, writing a story about the way you would like things to go allows the brain a visual of what you expect to happen.

On the reverse, tacky side of this train of thought is that we can picture worst-case scenarios in an effort to be prepared for what we feel we could handle.

Friend, remember the clean walls. Don't forget to picture all that white. There is nothing but white. God who supplies the light. There is nothing in the white space, so why are we fretting? Nothing has happened. You have no way of knowing what could happen. You are completely neutral in the present moment. Now then, if your house is actually on fire, run. But if you are worried your electricity might be shut off, it has not happened. So it doesn't exist. Think of only the purest of white. What is in that space, in that clearing, is the ability to stop, breathe, and ask, "Am I thinking, creating, or receiving?"

So let's say you can't pay your electric bill and the electricity is definitely going to be shut off.

Worrisome thinking is going to run on what-ifs and hypothetical solutions. And the cure to the panic is to pause, receive God's peace, and then do what you can. Take the next small step.

Identifying the threat is part of the thinking process. You currently have electricity. Breathe. Now do what needs to be done right now. Get some candles and a flashlight and light them. Make plans for dinner and get it ready. Call the electricity company and inquire about their emergency help to pay your bills. Call your church (or the church down the road) to see if they have a benevolence fund to help. Call the person who gifted you this book. Look into a shelter.

I don't know all your options, because I am not you. But I know my God. In the peace we were promised, he has made a way because he is wholly mixed into us. We are wholly eligible to be all he says we are, because of who he is.

As Christ followers, we say we believe, but we fall short of receiving peace simply because the noise—the news, social media, stinky theology, and worst-case scenarios—mix in with our thoughts, tainting the brilliance of a perfect match—us and our Creator.

Let's acknowledge we are transformed. Say it out loud in the mirror. We are different because he is mixed in with us. That blending cannot be undone, and nothing can separate us from love.

A perfect blend of love and wisdom whispering good plans to your heart.

THE FINISHING TOUCH

Jesus, I believe you. Worry and doubt are loud, but your shade and protection are a part of who I am. I cannot be removed from you, your love, or your wisdom. And by this truth I am at peace. Amen.

DAY 28

If Looks Could Kill

But the LORD helped me.
PSALM 118:13

Wouldn't it have been fun if in this devotional I could've announced, "We have found a house!"

I thought this would be that devotion. Because I thought we finally found our home. The images online were nothing short of darling. The professional drone footage of the pristinely manicured yard, mature trees, and walking trails through lush gardens was breathtaking. The interior had the midcentury elements I loved. Interior planters, built in shelves and cabinets, funky lights, and heavily textured wallpapers. The original travertine floors in the entry, halls, and bathrooms were immaculate. At first glance all I could think was, *This is my house. Finally this is our new home.*

It was fun to look at the house online and dream. But upon our arrival, with Justin's naysaying, construction-law-packed brain, things turned ugly fast. The house I loved in theory could have easily killed us in reality. It was a mess. The current owners were

self-proclaimed DIY folks. Only in this case, DIY did not stand for "do it yourself"—it stood for "death is yours if you don't step away from the power tools, fool."

Bless it, the house was a collection of carpenter ants holding hands, with a fresh coat of paint and a natural gas line that ran through the return-air vent. Just in case you want to asphyxiate your entire family. Unsuspecting house shoppers were met with a letter that read: "Home is being sold as is. All cash. No inspection. No appraisal."

In real estate and construction, this statement basically means that you should *not* buy this. You can't live here safely.

Many of the issues were cosmetic. However, many were dire. Such as, "Load-bearing walls in living and master removed by owner" and "No running water in bathrooms or utility room." Or my favorites, "Minor electrical shocks from kitchen light switches" and "Ghosts."

Yeah. Ghosts. While I don't subscribe to the idea of haunted houses, I appreciate the disclosure. Also, I don't buy "haunted houses" on principle.

But I want to testify, yet again, to the tangible safety of real companionship with Jesus. When we're in our Sunday best, teeth brushed, pantyhose pulled taut, and our Bibles tucked under our arms, we can practice the illusion of belief and a sound, reasonable Savior. But looking good and dazzling the Joneses with our "vibe" is just part of our physical aesthetic. It has no holding power. It is not the real safety of the promises of Christ.

In the case of the haunted house, it did look very pretty. But it was of no real value because it was a house of death. That is what we call it—the House of Death.

Oh, but isn't this just so descriptive of a believer in Jesus whose life is crashing down on her head? And she looks so good. But, shoog, we aren't safe in the comforts of the promises of Christ until we know and trust them.

It is possible to not just *look* like you are rocking this life—it is possible to *actually* live a life rocking everything you encounter. But right now, our gas lines may simply be running through the ventilation system.

We can get those lines rerouted and functioning at full capacity by actively addressing truth and separating it from the illusion. And yes, I want you to write it out. In this instance I learned that the images I had been excited by were not the truth. And I did that by physically going to the house and seeing it for myself. Some of our beliefs cannot be tested like that, but that doesn't mean we cannot find and experience them. I wrote out what I loved about the house, followed by, "Jesus, I would like to see more of those things I loved. Thank you for guiding me. Thank you for always opening my eyes to truth and your tangible companionship." And I could feel the companionship and safety in my bones. God is my help, no kidding—I believe it. God helps me. I trust him.

How has he helped you? Write about it!

THE FINISHING TOUCH

Jesus, when the weight is too heavy, wires are crossed, and I am out of resources, you always help me.
I like you. Amen.

Shades and Highlights

I have come into the world as a light, so that no one who believes in me should stay in darkness.

JOHN 12:46

As an author and artist, I will confess, science is not my jam. However, one day during the composition of my third book, *Well, Girl: An Inside-Out Journey to Wellness*, God gently prodded me down a *molecular* path. It made me itchy. I usually don't mix science and faith . . . until I realized the background of color theory. While color theory is the art of color . . . there is also the science of color that backs it. And, boy, did God make color interesting.

We humans see colors in light waves. Mixing red, green, and blue light sources of innumerable potencies allows us to create colors. The more light you add, the brighter and more intense the color mix becomes.

Did you catch that? In scientific light theory, white is a color—it is, in fact, all colors.

I can hear you saying, "Hold your crayons, sister. In kindergarten I scribbled all the colors over each other and got black."

And you'd be right. In pigments, white is the absence of color (that white space we talked about earlier), and black is what happens when you mix everything together.

But in light theory? Black is what happens when someone turns off the light. It's the absence of light.

Mind-blowing.

It's also important to note that color is a perception. When our eyes see something (such as grass), the object reflects light in different combinations of wavelengths, and the data for "green" is sent from our eyes to our brains. Our brains analyze those wavelength combinations and report the sightings as what we call color. So really the grass is every color, except for green. Interesting, right?

But beyond just the physical science of color, there's a whole level of psychological science associated with color. Colors are actually associated with feelings. And now we are talking about something that is not only my jam but combines science and faith.

I am convinced that science does have a place in our faith walk. When we understand and operate from an organized, intentionally designed mind space, we can use science to highlight and increase the intensity of our beliefs while simultaneously increasing our faith.

When I first met with my art agent and her graphic designer, the designer described to me what his role was in the process of published art for retail. If they wanted to list a piece of my work, he would scan it and upload it into Photoshop, recolor any discrepancies, and then add it to the catalog. However, he explained, "I can't clean up mud." Mud being the desaturated color that becomes muddied when a combination of colors on the palette mix together forming browns and grays and icky unintentional tones.

In spiritual terms the absence of light is associated with death, mourning, and darkness—the absence of God-created goodness. The presence of light (white containing all the colors), on the other hand, is symbolic of purity, innocence, light, hope, angels, and heaven—the presence of God's design. But the muddied spaces of our spiritual walk—those places we tend to forget about, that are unintentional or forgotten—are also significant. Like the designer said, mud is hard to clean, it stains, and runs all over things that would otherwise be sparkling, vivid, and clear. So how do we stop the muddy bleed in our lives?

Hide it under a bushel? Pretend it isn't there?

Nope.

Where there is light, darkness cannot hide. Where there is mud, there is a lack of clarity. We need clarity so that we might let in more light. Fear and doubt are best described as muddied spots in our faith development. What we see, hear, taste, touch, and experience add to the palette. Confusion and disappointment run haphazardly into what we held closely as hope. However, unlike the graphic designer who is unable to clean up muddied tinctures, we have the help of the Master Creator.

When we encounter a place in our lives that feels muddy and confusing—Do I take this job? How do I answer this nasty email?—we stop, implement our tools of gratitude, and ask ourselves the question we've come back to again and again this section: "Am I thinking, creating, or receiving?"

Intentionality is like a miracle Photoshop tool God designed. Stop and ask God to grant you clarity, thank him for how you know he'll show up, and then wait for your eyes to see the definite and infinite ways of earth as it is in heaven. You are thanking him in advance for answering your prayer for clear direction—because he will answer that question. Thanking him shows the subconscious, "Oh good. Thank you means it is done." From that heart-head space, the eyes are clear, solutions will come out of nowhere!

Look there! All the colors of peace.

THE FINISHING TOUCH

Oh, but you are a creative God! As I grow in my understanding of worry and strife, I acknowledge you are the answer. I give thanks for your wonders. I wait with joyful expectancy of all the light you bring to me. Amen.

Mind Makeover

We've continued to look to the light and spy the white. To further our ability to differentiate between panic, worry, and strife, use our question, "Am I thinking, creating, or receiving?" Please continue to use this question as a breath prayer in the coming days. I invite you to write, doodle, color, script, print, and draw thoughts and prayers as a way to even further stimulate change.

Look at you, so crisp and cool!

SECTION FOUR
Back in the Black

Enter Here

*For anyone who enters God's rest also rests from
their works, just as God did from his.*

HEBREWS 4:10

I feel the world would be lackluster without the helpful hues of light and deep, rich shades and shadows of darkness. While white is the definitive accent of cleanliness, black plays an equal part in defining things like elegant dinner attire and celebrations of life after losing a loved one.

As discussed in the previous section, a current popular trend is the white industrial farmhouse design. The crispiness of white in contrast to galvanized or antiqued metals and rough cuts and dated wood elements create a light yet warm aesthetic.

In contrast, black is always closely tied to a more elegant, formal design plan. Sleek black cabinets or a reflective black floor lends to a modern, techy feel. Clean lines and minimal accents together with smooth black surfaces are also interpreted as cool and edgy. However, black can also be used in farmhouse designs. A bold black-and-white buffalo print is considered country chic without being brash or outdated. No need to hearken back to the mideighties and the early nineties, when black-and-white interior decor was symbolic of a "righteous" design. Checkerboard patterns decorated our Vans as the melodies of Michael Jackson and Blondie hummed totally awesome jams over our boom boxes.

If you mix white and black, you'll find a gray that is also the rage on the farm and in the city. Sleek, shiny, reflective gray surfaces can offer the same polished finishes as modern-day sheeny black designs. In more rustic designs, gray highlights baskets, fixtures, and refurbished pieces without demanding or distracting from their statements. Gray also can be used to age certain pieces or aspects of a design. A cool gray-blue front door implies a calm, relaxed, and serene human dwelling behind the door. Gray is traditional, without the formalness of black or the blatant suggestion of stark white. While the mix of white and black can be useful in design, gray is culturally associated with stormy weather, depressed moods, and uncertainty.

There can be no doubt about the certainty of black and white. But gray? No one wants to live in unsettled gray indefinitely.

Wouldn't it be amazing if our lives avoided the depressed moods and uncertainty of gray? While some areas of our lives seem grayer than others, the Bible assures us that we have clearly defined black and white lines in our journeys here on earth. This is the good news.

When things are gray—and we wonder, "Do I go this way? Or

that?"—that's when we can call on our life overhaul contractor, Jesus, to help draw the black and white lines. When society changes the rules and suddenly white is okay after Labor Day and checkerboard sneakers are once again "Dude!," we can trust that God will clearly show us which way to go in life.

You might find yourself saying, "I can't tell what God wants. I can never decipher my voice from his." I would like to step onto my soapbox and remind us that we *can* do all things through Christ, who is our strength, and *can't* only wins when we believe it can. Give no power to your *can't*.

There are no gray areas in the promises of Jesus. You can hear his voice. It may not look or sound like I hear God's voice, and it may not look or sound like how your best friend or grandma's first cousin hears God's voice, but he is speaking, and you can hear it with some practice.

Grab your pen and paper again and write, "I choose to believe you are speaking. Today I will look for you in other people and in the creation around me." Then purposefully look for God. Every time you see the color black today, take it as God's whisper that he sees you.

If you're in the midst of trying to make a decision, rest in the promise that God will lead you. If you haven't heard new direction, keep moving forward until he draws you a new line.

THE FINISHING TOUCH

Jesus, you light the shadows and bring the daylight to the darkness.
In areas of confusion and lack, you are the brightness and joy
I expect. Hallelujah! Amen.

Good Bones

*To them God has chosen to make known among the Gentiles
the glorious riches of this mystery, which is Christ in you,
the hope of glory.*

COLOSSIANS 1:27

In renovation and DIY, there's a phrase we say that gets our creative juices hoppin'—"It has good bones." Sure, there may be some wood rot, and this wall may need to go or be moved over a smidge. But in general, if the structure has good bones, I can make it good as new.

I am here to testify that you, as a believer, are more than the dry rot of worry and the bad walls of depression. Your bones are not just good—you have Christ in you, the hope of glory. And uncovering that is the most desirable and intoxicating part of your life remodel.

The truth of who he is and why he died is all the security we need to proceed in living a glorious life. This is the good news. It is not "sort of okay" news. It is *good news*. No other shoe will drop.

Unfortunately, just because we have good bones—the strength of a loving God standing behind us—doesn't mean we *believe* we have good bones.

If I say I think your sofa is ugly, it does

you no harm unless you believe (practice the thought) that my opinion matters to your safety and well-being.

When we read our Bibles as law instead of allowing the Holy Spirit to flow through it and in us, we allow all the shoulds, shouldn'ts, woulds, and wouldn'ts to build an ugly wall over the good. Stop shoulding on yourself.

When it comes to churchy words and religious law, it is imperative to know the truth of and what you feel about a teaching or practice before you install it as a fixture in your life. There was a time I believed I was full of demons and needed to be cleansed. I paid big bucks, chanted big prayers. And I gave power to the teaching that I was somehow stained with the sins of my past, even though I had been saved. I rehearsed the feelings of darkness, and I practiced them until I was a broken, rotted shell of a woman. Now I don't believe that ritualistic, sacrificial displays do anything for your status as a saved and beloved child of God.

Shoog, don't go back to the dry rot when Jesus gives you a sparkling mansion.

Jesus overcame everything in the world—including everything in your life. We are here to get to the good bones of the good news and get rid of any lies of lack.

Stop rehearsing the prayers of the broken. I propose that we have given power to the pulpit, pews, and stained-glass windows, paid homage to the people and the teachings, learned and believed the salvation work wasn't finished. And this is the dry rot going on behind the scenes.

But Jesus gave you good bones—bones that don't rot no matter the circumstances, no matter the trials, and no matter what anyone else says.

Let go of the beliefs religion has placed on you. Let no person, search engine, or media trend decide who you are. Instead believe that you are bought and paid for. When we receive that good news of God, we receive the gloriously juicy fruit of the Spirit: "love, joy, peace, forbearance, kindness, goodness, faithfulness, gentleness and self-control" (Galatians 5:22–23).

These are gifts already promised us. All you have to do is receive those good bones. So if you're struggling with kindness, get somewhere quiet for a second, then say, "With the Holy Spirit, I am kind today." Feel free to ignore what religion says is kind and listen for God's whisper of how to be kind, and choose to do it. Or if you're struggling with peace, say, "With the Holy Spirit, today I will find peace." Then choose to let the light of peace flood through you.

THE FINISHING TOUCH

Jesus, I want to see things through the eyes of your "yes!" Today I need your guidance in play. With the mind of a child, I want to experience the blessing of more by increasing my faith in you rather than toiling with the burdens of my limits. I wait with eager expectation for the big reveal! Amen.

Factory Installed Security System

*Then you will know the truth,
and the truth will set you free.*

JOHN 8:32

I can't be held responsible for punching someone in the throat if they had the bright idea to pop up out of nowhere and yell, "Boo!"

Not cool.

These types of antics are no-no's at my house. However, as a mom, I can fully expect to still get freaked out by my children, as they too are uniquely designed. During the composition of this book, our nine-year-old, Sam, wandered into my bedroom, having had a nightmare.

Like any good parent, I rubbed his back. "Do you want to talk about the dream?" Unfortunately, he did. Sam explained through tear-filled eyes that he dreamed a puppet was standing outside his bedroom window howling, "Saammm! Saammm!"

But if that doesn't have you freaked out, he went on to tell me that he then rolled over to wake up his younger brother, only to find Charlie was a puppet too.

I cooed my heartfelt apologies to Sam for the terror, all the while my insides screaming, "NOOOOOOO! No puppets or clowns."

But it was on the next night that I intervened in what could have become a lifelong fostered fear. Sam didn't want to sleep in his room. Every shadow, every bump in the night triggered the puppet memory, raising the chemical responses in his little body, causing more fear and angst. I won't lie—after his nightmare, I was pretty worked up too.

I reminded Sam about his custom settings for healthy fear responses. Yes, if it were possible that a crazed killer ventriloquist's puppet could be on the loose terrorizing citizens, it would be wise to acknowledge every thump in the night. But I checked the news, and there was no report of such disturbances. I went on to explain why Sam was so quick to spot suspicious shadows and hear weird creaks and bumps.

The conscious mind, the part of your brain reading this now, might remember the dream. It is also receiving my suggestions. The heart-head part remembers the dream too. But it also remembers the *feelings* of having been threatened by the puppet. The heart-head cannot differentiate between the real and the imagined. This is why Olympic athletes watch videos and visualize perfect events. Their subconscious believes that they actually experienced the big win and can more readily stimulate the physical body to repeat the same eloquent execution. As with any good design, this was made intentionally. God designed the brain to have the RAS, or reticular activating system.

Think of RAS as the security video surveillance of your mind. The RAS is a group of cells at the base of the brain that acts as a filter for what is and isn't relevant for your brain to process. The interesting thing is that RAS assesses your feelings (not facts) when checking your surroundings. Then it uses that somewhat unreliable information to decide whether to alert your subconscious to pay attention. So if the RAS is on high alert for another incident of puppet terror, it will alert the subconscious of every subtle movement or sound.[6] Even though it didn't feel good to be afraid, the subconscious doesn't want to be terrorized by Chucky or any of his cohorts.

The creaky floor may have always creaked, but before the puppet in the window incident, the RAS didn't have any reason to report the sound to the subconscious. Floors creak—sleep on, little one. But now, based on the relevance of things that *should not be*, the RAS screams to the subconscious, "Did you hear that?"

Yes, it did hear it, because the RAS allowed the sound through as a warning.

Take a deep breath, lovely. Then think about situations, people, and places that tend to trigger your panic. What is the truth behind the panic? Real panic means real trouble to our bodies. Yes, this practice of evaluating panic responses can quickly get away from us, but even then, it's not a bad thing that we were created to physically react. Go with that. Breathe. You are not in trouble. If you feel sick with worry, you are seen, heard, and known. And when you are not in panic, you can use your feel-good feelings—maybe try gratitude. But do some preplanning for the truth you want to feel. Look up some verses about how strong and loving God is.

I'll go first: "For the Spirit God gave us does not make us timid, but gives us *power, love* and *self-discipline*" (2 Timothy 1:7, emphasis mine).

THE FINISHING TOUCH

Jesus, I can choose to be afraid, or I can choose to be at rest, because my design is so perfectly fashioned. There is room to teach my mind new tricks. Thank you. Amen.

DAY 34

Traditionally Speaking

*Jesus Christ is the same yesterday
and today and forever.*

HEBREWS 13:8

Black decor comes and goes. During the planning of this book, I thought there would be no room for current black decor. And then just as I crossed it off my list, my art agent sent me retail call-out sheets from buyers, and lo and behold, black is back. In fact, black siding with gray or white trim and a bold front door is just coming into popularity. Black is a traditional, classy look for a front door, a roof, or as a contrasting shade.

Traditional architecture and design is exactly as you would expect: a warm, classic, comforting, familiar home and decor style grounded in tradition without being set in any particular time period. Traditional decor could include a neutral color palette, carved wood, or upholstered furnishings. Many of us grew up in homes that could be classified as traditional, which is the reason so many of us feel most at home in places with traditional decor. Granted, we are often swayed by the latest trend. Don't fret, but apparently this next generation is referring to "traditional" design as "granny chic."

So if your home looks like a museum or Nana's house, you're still just as hip as we both first suspected. You needn't even get rid of that weird lamp that Aunt Clara bequeathed you. I am certain it looks fantastic . . . exactly as expected and therefore comfortable.

Expectation is knowing something is a certain way and can be trusted. If you haven't fully arrived in the safety and comfort of what you can count on, changing your mind means identifying the space that still holds the doubts of the past and actively expecting it to change into that which brings you rest.

You can expect your home to look and run a certain or traditional way. But if you make no effort to experience and feel changes, it is nearly impossible to implement them in ways that become habitual.

Let's say you live in a suburb of New York, on a half acre of parklike bliss. Five bedrooms, four bathrooms, gourmet kitchen, the works. Then you decide you're tired of the long commute and traffic. You decide to reinvent your life, move to the city, sell your car, and settle into a three-bedroom, two-bath, high-rise apartment.

You go from traditional eclectic to contemporary and enjoy watching the sunset through the skyscrapers. But at zero hour, you decide to

keep your car. Now, all the changes have been made, except . . . you are still sitting in standstill traffic two hours a day.

You justify—"I might need the car." Then you reanalyze—"I need to make the parking fees worth it, so I will still drive to work." But the initial issue of a commute was the reason for the change. Why did you only go part of the distance?

Because the car is what you know and expect.

It's the same thing with your life. If you continue to expect your to-do list, your money, and your friends to bail you out of life's circumstances and get you where you need to go, you'll be sitting in a traffic jam of stress.

Talk about expecting to be stressed! But, shoog, that's not the design you were created to experience. Expectation goes two ways. We can ask and expect God's help.

What things are you expecting to help you through your stress? Can you see how holding on to those is just throwing you in the midst of a traffic jam? Start a practice of telling God you expect him to show up. Tonight tell God you expect him to show up. Wake up tomorrow and keep a list of the good things in your life.

THE FINISHING TOUCH

Father, I know you know me. You know how I roll, and you know the things I would like to change. I am falling headlong into your arms, and I fully expect to be held. Thank you for your protective care and attention. Amen.

DAY 35

Mind Makeover

We've learned about the RAS and our delightful and intentional design, which never goes out of style. I would like you to be aware of what you are noticing and what makes you feel panicky. Is your security system on high alert? Are you repeatedly seeing shadows when the light is right beside you? Use your breath and oxygenate the body and say one of these Mind Makeover prayers until it is habit.

 I see clearly now. No harm will come to me.

I choose an organized mind and to align my heart-head with the positive words of my mouth.

 I expect you to show up.

DAY 36

Decisions, Decisions

*In all your ways acknowledge him,
and he will make straight your paths.*

PROVERBS 3:6 ESV

While studying family and consumer sciences at Abilene Christian University in 1993, I had the privilege of taking several interior design classes. I say *privilege* because the study of family and consumer science encompassed all the aspects of home—a subject I adore. Studying decor was an exhilarating experience because how we feel at home matters.

I had no trouble deciding to study a subject that centered around family, food, finance, furniture, parenting, child development, textiles, and geriatrics. To me this was, and still is, the good stuff. For a brief moment, I considered abandoning my home economics major and switching to an interior design major. Alas, the one-direction curriculum was entirely too monochromatic for me.

Still, for a season, the appeal of owning my own design studio, decorating elaborate rooms, and shopping with someone else's money enticed

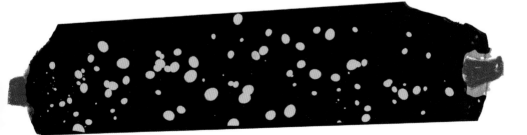

me to consider the degree. It was in the fall of my sophomore year that my adviser said, "Jami, you are going to have to decide." I worried I would never be satisfied with "just decorating." Yet my 4.0 GPA was bumped to a 3.8 only because of my incapability in the sewing room. I grappled with the decision.

Let's be clear. Grappling (hand-to-hand combat with a decision) is worry. It is stressful and most often stems from the belief we will miss out on one thing for another or that we will make the wrong decision. In the end, I decided to stay the course with a degree in vocational family and consumer sciences. At the time, I believed I was giving up on one dream, but in reality I haven't missed an opportunity.

Instead I choose to believe in a loving God who gives me clear guidance. I declare and acknowledge he has a design for my life that is stress-free.

Imagine your half bath was completely black. The pedestal sink, the toilet, the marble tile walls, the fixtures—all are black. You call in a specialist. A week later you return to your new bathroom. The walls are still shiny black marble. But the sink and toilet are a crisp, modern white with shiny, sharp-edged brass fixtures. The mirror is now an eclectic midcentury-modern gold starburst. And the light fixtures are simple Edison bulbs on hanging wires. A wild palm plant in a brass bucket brings one corner to life. And a sleek maple shelf opposite the plant boasts crisp white hand towels, a white linen candle, and fancy soaps no one will ever use.

Will you switch back to the all black? Not a chance. You move into the new space and revel in the perfection. And your prayers? You state your need, struggle, and want and then move into a new lighter mind space. You'll notice that not all the black is gone, but that is no longer the focus. In life we don't know what's coming around the corner. But as we learned in day 34, we can expect God to show up. We can turn our thinking and creating into receiving.

Furthermore, the belief that we are unable to decide is a declaration of lack. Statements such as "I can't decide" or "I never know what to do" testify to the mind the opposite of what is truth—Christ is in us, and he knows the truth of who we are and our abilities. If we are seeking him, he will never let us miss our calling.

Rewrite common statements such as "My boss is killing me" and "My kid is a pain in the neck" into positive statements and gratitude declarations to activate the change from stressed to blessed. For example, "My boss expects a lot. He is intent on making the company successful." Or, "My child is complaining more than I would like. We need to sit down and talk through some things." See how we can improve our communication? When we ask questions or write out a better thought, the mind goes to work on that.

THE FINISHING TOUCH

Lord God, I acknowledge that you make all things new. I seek more of your wisdom and love. I believe you direct my steps as a mother directs her child. Help me trust you as I decide what is for me and what is not. Amen.

DAY 37

A Minimal(ist)

And be thankful.

COLOSSIANS 3:15

When it comes to Jesus, I'm a card-carrying, committed minimalist. For years I acted as if Jesus wanted to be hard on me. I added to his singular command, "Love," and smashed my head against the rotted walls of worry and distress. I stressed over my lack, which he had called blessed (Matthew 5:3), and tried harder than hard to make him love me by making the easy promises of Christ the impossible work of religion.

In minimalist design, or "organic modern," simplicity is emphasized with monochromatic color choices, clean lines, natural fabrics, and the philosophy less is more. But creating a true minimalist decor is not as effortless as a couch on one wall and a bare table on the other.

But I imagine minimalism is an excellent stress reducer. I picture a gal with a heart for the simple who knows where the scissors are in her home. I know we have scissors . . . somewhere.

While minimal might not appeal to all—let's be honest, the ease and cleanliness are incomparable—many of us have too much stuff we deem important and necessary to move to a minimalist style. I got a bee up my skirt one time to redecorate a room in minimalist fashion. It didn't work out. I have things I like to collect and paintings either I can't part with or no one else can possibly understand. When I can't explain why I painted a giraffe with a pet goldfish, it's easier to assume that painting was just for me and to hang it next to dozens of other unexplainable works. The eclectic suits me, and my random collection brings me joy.

Unlike the minimalist style, an attitude of gratitude works for everyone. Even science agrees. The verbal, written, or mental exercise of giving thanks actually releases dopamine.[7] This feel-good hormone notifies the subconscious. *Hey, she doesn't have a care in the world!* It's both a simple form of worship *and* a great stress reducer. Win-win.

Seasonally, I have lived a minimalist lifestyle. I was raised in hotels and campgrounds. Granted, we had homes along the way. But as my dad worked his way up the corporate ladder, we moved more often than we stayed. The antics, near misses, and afflictions that my family encountered as we moved more south than our northern roots might have been comfortable with could easily fill a book. My dad, the primordial optimist, neglected weather alerts and no-camping signs and considered one-star reviewed motels as an opportunity for adventure rather than a warning of impending disaster.

However, I never recall feeling the pangs of homelessness. Perhaps because I knew the situations were temporary and not the totality of our existence. We would stay at one roadside inn until we found our next temporary housing, and then we would move out of that and into a tent while we went in search of the next. I trusted my parents to care for me and my siblings. Trust is a big stepping stone, or brick paver, leading to a lighthearted, stress-free life.

Like I trusted my loving parents, we can trust our Father to move us to safety and rest. Our struggles and temporary worldly experiences are of relevance to a good and faithful creator. He knows when we are suffering and in need, and he doesn't neglect us. Make his faithfulness your minimalist focus. Use gratitude to fuel your trust.

Gratitude for what makes you feel good flips the switch on the complexities of worry and forces the mind into a state of *Ahhhh . . . that was simple.*

To put this into practice, consider memorizing some Scripture to help combat those ugly thoughts. Consider writing one of the following verses on an index card:

"Because you've always stood up for me, I'm free to run and play. I hold on to you for dear life, and you hold me steady as a post" (Psalm 63:7–8 MSG).

"Those who trust in the LORD are like Mount Zion, which cannot be shaken but endures forever" (Psalm 125:1).

Take the index card with you while you go do something you truly enjoy—going for a walk, reading in a favorite nook, shooting hoops at the gym, or visiting with friends at a local coffee shop.

THE FINISHING TOUCH

I am simply grateful that you are my loving Father. I want to use gratitude to change my mind, and I want to constantly give thanks for that which is good, pure, and holy. I am so thankful and simply blessed by you who loves me. Amen.

DAY 38

Poor Air Quality

*Don't be fooled by those who say such things, for
"bad company corrupts good character."*

1 CORINTHIANS 15:33 NLT

Because my father-in-law was an HVAC expert, we have some precisely crafted clean air. With two little boys running around, nonstinky air is a running joke in our family. But in reality, lack of clean air can be a serious issue. Poor air quality can impact your life, even endanger or end it.

Here's one example. We obviously need air to live. But sometimes carbon monoxide is in the air. An abudance of carbon monoxide, which is tasteless and odorless, is deadly. Years ago a family in Justin's hometown was remodeling their home. The husband of the family had some construction experience and a smidgen of knowledge as to how electrical components are connected. In the process of the remodel, he needed to move the HVAC unit to a different location. Insisting he could do it himself, he asked for some general directions and purchased some ductwork and a thermostat.

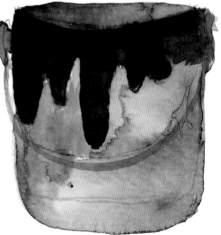

All was well and the home was finished that fall. But when winter rolled around, the family got sick.

Spring arrived, and they felt better. And when winter rolled around, they got sick again. This went on for a few years. The husband called Justin's family's shop and said, "Could you guys come over to check our heater? Something is not right. The key is under the mat. My wife is home, but she's really sick. She can't get out of bed and is barely able to be awakened. You won't bother her."

Well, if it was a bother for her, it saved her life.

When Justin and his dad, Gene, arrived, she was minutes away from expiring. They called the fire department after they carried the poisoned woman from her would-be deathbed. During the remodel years before, when the heater was relocated, it was not properly installed. It had been leaking carbon monoxide into the home. The air she lived in every day of winter almost killed her.

And it isn't just clean physical air that we need. We need pure spiritual air too.

Far too often we've stayed in our tiny quarters, plagued by the black smog of our worries with only our shallow panting to carry us through. We've struck at Jesus as he's tried to carry us out of the choking air because we believed the lie that Jesus will turn away when we do something wrong. But displacing Jesus with wrong beliefs only leads to worsening symptoms. The internal struggles lead to our physical breaths growing more desperate and jagged, leaving our bodies in a heap of stress.

In the Bible God is called the breath of life. Doesn't that sound heavenly? Deep breathing and increasing the amount of oxygen in your brain signals your parasympathetic nervous system, thereby making you calm.[8]

So when we feel stressed, when we're confronted with something that spikes our adrenaline and makes us question our lives and our God, let's run for the clean air of the Jesus we see in the Bible. If someone tells us that we can do something to make Jesus hate us, let's look to the Bible, where he tells us he is the very definition of love. Let's see the stories where he hung out with those who struggled to find the right path.

Come to the party, friend. Explore, be enriched, and be enlightened! Where fear and worry were once the dilapidated remains of your day, now let peace and rest delight.

How, you ask?

Stop.

Breathe.

Let the peace and power of the Holy Spirit fill your nostrils. Feel it as it warms and expands your precious lungs. Imagine it as it effortlessly separates into what is for you and what is not. You cannot be separated from the peace you need.

Now exhale. Let go of the disappointment and the past and then . . . take more air. There is plenty. Thank the Holy Spirit for the breath of life. And exhale again. Focus on the breathing and away from the worries.

Acknowledge you don't have to worry about that anymore, you enchanting hippie.

THE FINISHING TOUCH

I breathe in your peace and exhale my angst. You fill me until I overflow with goodness and mercy. I acknowledge the power of my creation and relish in the peace that your Holy Spirit continually breathes into me. Amen.

DAY 39

Best Idea EVER!

And we know that in all things God works for the good of those who love him, who have been called according to his purpose.

ROMANS 8:28

During the construction of our traditional saltbox home, high on a hill overlooking our ranch, I had what I thought was the best idea ever, for the billionth time. I was out for dinner with some girlfriends, and one of them suggested we stroll around downtown to see all the new goodies in our favorite stores.

One shop was an eclectic furniture store with unusual pieces from all over the world. Since I had a small furniture budget for our new home, I was eager to see what I could find. The two-story retail shop had a "secret" attic space with discounted pieces, and this was my favorite spot to look for treasure. As my friends wandered downstairs, sipping wine and visiting with the owner, I scurried up the old side staircase in search of, well, nothing in particular.

And that is when I saw it. An antique bar, something you would find in an old tavern in some lonely Mexican village, with aged nail heads and distinctive scratches, wear, and tear. Up until this point my husband and I had been poring over bids from cabinetmakers and trim carpenters, but this tattered old bar inspired an idea.

No cabinets.

That's right—no cabinets. I called Justin. The next day he and I wandered through the store picking out pieces of furniture in lieu of permanent cabinets. Then we ventured to an antique store where we bought armoires to serve as linen closets and other storage. And our frugality and enthusiasm for the idea had an added bonus—we would be saving nearly twenty thousand dollars in trim carpentry.

Open shelves with colorful plates, cobalt-blue ice-tea tumblers, and trendy bowl sinks atop aged, repurposed cupboards and chests added character to the new build, while simultaneously saving money and creating something that was a showstopper.

Until one day when I found the inconvenience of having no cabinets more burdensome than the lovely atmosphere of furniture pieces I had created. It looked amazing, but it was hardly convenient. And I was frustrated with the clutter. The bottom line was, it didn't work as good as it looked.

So we sold several of the pieces and eventually had real kitchen cabinets installed. The original antique bar was the only piece that stayed. We picked paint-grade cabinets, and Justin painted them a rich flat black. Then I added mismatched glass, brass, and copper handles and drawer pulls. The counters were covered in three-inch terra-cotta tiles, and I created a whimsical backsplash out of marbles, bottle tops, and sea glass.

And many voiced their preference for the old design.

However, I had learned something. I learned I need the luxury of a modern kitchen. The pioneers didn't have nine hundred pieces of Tupperware with eighteen hundred lids that did not fit any of the containers. How did I learn this? I felt the angst and frustration associated with my first design.

Our best ideas don't always work out, and we learn from our experiences. In our home, we have the saying, "Failure is always an option." I have said this for years to our children, and they will say it helped. But I say it to myself even more. Because it's okay to try and miss the mark. It's okay to be disappointed. And it's okay to try something new or close the door on an idea simply because you have been led to move on.

It's okay.

It's okay.

It is always okay.

I confess—I just giggled in real life. This little gem of a phrase has been so life changing for me and my family that my heart-head gets a little lighter and I can feel the physical change of the words "It's okay."

I invite you to write out a few words about the statement "It's okay." Be specific. In what area are you struggling? Then write, "It's okay." Have you been working to control your temper and lost it yesterday? It's okay. Did that business venture not turn out how you dreamed? It's okay. That choice you made, that place you went, that dream you miss. It's okay. Think about these words. How assuring are they to you? In an emergency, these are often the words we crave to hear—"It's okay." Say these words, write them, think them, and feel them.

Um, I am pretty sure this is the best idea ever.

THE FINISHING TOUCH

Thank you, Jesus, that it's okay. It is always okay! Amen.

DAY 40

Mind Makeover

While minimalist decorating may not be easy and might not be for everyone, that clean, simple, airy feel is exactly what God intends for our heart-heads. What practices of worry have you thought are just "how you are"? In an effort to change the words of our mouths into perfect alignment with the deep beliefs in our heart-heads, it is imperative we acknowledge and *experience* that we are new and that we were wonderfully and perfectly designed.

This week note your breath. What is the spiritual air quality when you are racked with fostered fears and continued terrors? Write out your favorite Scripture from this section, and keep it in your pocket. When you notice your breath tightening and worry pinging in your mind, stop. Choose to receive rather than think or create. Clear the fogginess through deep cleansing breaths and then read the Scripture out loud. Feel the feelings of peace and attribute them to the light.

I picked this one: "Then you will know the truth, and the truth will set you free" (John 8:32).

Breathe out all the dark and breathe in the light.

SECTION FIVE

Feeling Blue

DAY 41

Feeling Blue

*In the beginning God created
the heavens and the earth.*

GENESIS 1:1

If home is your refuge and you wish to reside in serenity, a blue door is the door for you. Some speculate that some Amish paint their doors blue when they have a daughter ready to be wed. It's a sign of welcome. How's that for an old-school dating app? Whether or not you are interested in luring suitors to your daughter's porch swing, you might like a blue door because historically blue has been a symbol of all that is good in life. Water and the sky are blue, and often the air we breathe is symbolized with blue. That may be why it's my favorite color.

In Mediterranean design, blue and white are not only a nod to the vast Aegean Sea, but regional regulations also require those colors to be the central palette for building. The regulations are in place to prevent anything that might distract from the breathtaking blues of the waves and to keep the cities and villages alive with natural occurrences of stunning.

You won't catch me arguing with them.

The fact is that God created blue with the intent to arrest us. This leaves me undone. He knew we had the potential to be stopped in our tracks, look up or out, and be left in awe of the One who created sharp contrasts of piercing blue sky and fluffy white clouds, turquoise sea, and foamy waves. He alone decorates with blues in things like feathers, cobalt waters, and the bold navy of night.

While the reflective properties of sky and sea are life-giving, the use of the word *blue* in our culture is often correlated with the feeling of sadness or depression.

It's unfortunate that when we say, "I feel blue" or "I've got the blues," we negatively associate God's beautiful color with strife.

We've taken God's design for blue and twisted it just like we've taken the word *never*—which he uses to say he will never leave, never stop loving us, never stop pursuing us—and twisted it. Instead of seeing and acknowledging God's love, we say words of lack and limitation: "It will never work" and "Never in a million years will I be able to . . ."

Just as we associate blue with depression and a lousy mood, we use the word *never* in a way that can confuse the mind, making your heart-head renovation a flop. When negative associations are attached to a word, negative feelings pop up, causing us to believe we have issues in our design.

For instance, we say, "I will never doubt the love of Jesus." And the heart-head volleys back. "Really? Never? What about that time . . ." And then we are forced to recount doubt, making us feel depressed, reluctant, and . . . blue.

Shoog, our nevers and the world's nevers are not for us, the ones he calls his beloved—*always*.

Let's demo those never habits!

I try not to use the term "feeling blue" because, for me, the color doesn't correspond to a depressive state. What about the word *never*? Do you use it to hold yourself back or beat yourself up? Instead write out some of God's nevers and turn the blues into a hue you can rejoice in.

THE FINISHING TOUCH

Father, there are words in my culture that do not convey the truth of who you are or who you say I am. I acknowledge and give thanks for all you created for good. I come to you today prepared to give thanks for your goodness and vibrancy. I love you. Amen.

DAY 42

Trust the Process

*When I am afraid,
I put my trust in you.*

PSALM 56:3

In May 1992 I was a nineteen-year-old bride. Justin had just graduated from college. I didn't think about where we might live or what I might do when I grew up. I made no provisions for the future outside of being crazy in love.

Looking back, it was an idealistic way to live. I paid no mind to bills, and I felt no pressure to pick a career or have a baby. I was just blissfully obsessed with being the wife of Justin Gene Amerine.

So while I tied bridesmaid bouquets and attended wedding-dress fittings, Justin, a mature twenty-two-year-old, made bigger plans, plans for our future. With an oblivious bride chasing behind him, Justin went to work with his dad. My father-in-law, Gene, had built a successful air-conditioning business in the early 1960s. The wrathful West Texas heat and Gene's outstanding work ethic had turned the little company into a lucrative mechanical contracting corporation that provided for Gene, his wife, their three children, and eventually Justin, me, and our children.

Justin's dad found us a "deal" rental home. The owners, who had been stationed at the nearby air force base, were being sent overseas for two years. The 1920s home was a project the couple had taken on prior to their deployment.

Who better to care for their home than newlyweds with experience in construction? So we moved into a little blue house at the edge of town.

If being newly married to the dashing Justin was a dream come true, the little blue house in the middle of nowhere was a nightmare made real.

Something died under the porch, and the pungent stench of death became our norm. I held my breath as Justin carried me across the threshold. The plumbing worked . . . sometimes. There were rattlesnakes, which were probably attracted to the property by the overwhelming population of mice. The Sheetrock had been pulled off, exposing aged shiplap.

Who knew shiplap would become a thing? I assumed it was a nod to our poverty.

Suddenly, I went from wedded bliss to disgruntled stress and slipped into the depressive blue state of my new reality.

Twenty-nine years later, as I sit in my spacious office/studio hundreds of miles from that little starter home, overlooking a Houston pine forest, I wish I had trusted the process. Those were steps that brought me here, and had you witnessed them, you would have seen what a wreck I was, making the transformation all the more stunning.

This seems like another stressor, *transforming*. Especially in the struggle of real anxiety. How do you trust the process when you can't remember what started the anxious thoughts that ramped into a full-blown panic attack? Usually I couldn't remember. But really, isn't that part of the cyclical defeat of worry? Trying to pinpoint the problem, the root cause. In many cases this only caused me to rehash past catastrophes, resulting in a surge of stress hormones, regret, shame, and blame.

Blame is a form of judgment. It analyzes stress at the expense of forward movement. Stop. Right now, in this moment, right where you are, right this second. What do you feel? As we trust the process, we can map the thoughts on paper instead of just randomly letting them run wild. When we have a tangible, readable outline of those thoughts, we can physically see and feel the process through the movement of our pen across the paper. That process, that intentional 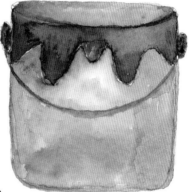 process, can be completed with a best-case scenario, our personal faith, on paper. The substance of things hoped for? There is your process.

Dear one, trust the process. Believe as if you have received. Let go of the unknown and the past, and look up and acknowledge you are seen, heard, and known. Write out a process from the past that had a good outcome. What did you miss along the way? Tell the subconscious, the heart-head, what you want to see and how you want to feel. This direction allows you to be part of the process rather than a helpless watcher.

THE FINISHING TOUCH

Jesus, I trust you. I acknowledge your goodness and your ways.
I trust the road I am walking is known by you. Help me grow in my
understanding of trust. I cast my worries, even the real stinky
ones, on your capable shoulders. Amen.

DAY 43

Flooring Options

*Show me your ways, LORD,
teach me your paths.*

PSALM 25:4

A s we start to become stripped of our old worrying ways, we can now start the fun part: decorating our environment with the aesthetic functionality of flooring. With drywall in place, before our trim carpenter does all the fine details, let us intentionally pick where we will tread and surround ourselves with that which is pleasing and comforting.

Floor and wall coverings, paint colors, wallpaper, or a troweled treatment are personal preferences. Not the law. Really, there is no law in what makes you feel safe, well, seen, heard, and known. If it doesn't work for you, it is of no value.

Recently, my husband and I decided that with the current seller's market, it makes no sense for us to sit on a paid-for house that is not pleasing to us anymore. With four older children out on their own, the size, configuration, and lack of yard space have negated the joy we felt when we first moved in.

And since we have been on the hunt for over a year for a new home, we've opted to sell ours and move into a temporary rental while we decide where we will land next. I love this idea. Justin, well, it puts a wobble in his swagger. I moved nineteen times before I graduated from high school. I like fresh starts and new locations simply because that is what I am accustomed to. Justin was born and raised in a small town in West Texas. He graduated with fifty high school classmates. He went to college an hour away, returning home on weekends to help his dad on the farm. And while we make decisions together, it's easier for me to pick up and go than it is for Justin.

And here's the thing. The fact that we don't approach things the same way is okay. Rather than giving power to indecisiveness and worries, acknowledging our differences adds to the ease of discussing and seeing our options. You might not be a natural matcher of texture and light. That's okay. Enlist the help of others.

However, we don't need a second or third opinion from without when we are equipped with the most durable, stain-resistant intelligence in creation—God himself.

When we look to the world outside us for answers, we may not like the aesthetic of the answer. In fact, the answer may conflict, may not be what we really need, or may lay on guilt and shame . . . all of which will send our heart-heads into a panic.

But when we stop and ask ourselves, "Am I thinking, creating, or receiving?" and then wait for the answer, we are operating from a God perspective (within). We are making decisions from a place of clarity, creativity, and divine inspiration.

On the other hand, if we go searching for advice from the outside world, things may trigger us or make us feel icky—like turquoise-blue-and-gold shag carpet. Though popular years ago, now such a matted mess of wear and tear makes me want to run screaming. Of course, you might call it retro and have a fun feeling when you tiptoe through the fibers, but those feelings are yours. You cannot transfer them to me, and we do not get to decide what others find pleasing.

See? What's good for you is not necessarily good for me. But if I were deciding what flooring to install (or job to take or how to discipline my toddler) and consulted someone who loves shag (or takes jobs strictly for the money or doesn't have kids), I'm potentially in for a world of confusion and frustration.

We can use this practice of aligning our thoughts into an organized, stress-free space when we go inside ourselves and look around and ask, "Am I thinking, creating, or receiving?" Then take it one step further by assessing, Is my solution from the outside world? Or am I trusting Christ in me? Without or within? That space has divine options and the durability to last the ages.

Today think through the people you typically ask for advice. Are they people who listen to God? Can you trust that they're seeking his will for your life? If not, pray and ask God to send godly people into your life. Then make a plan to go for coffee or a walk, play golf, or whatever activities the two of you may enjoy.

THE FINISHING TOUCH

Lord, I change my prayer. I am without nothing I need at this moment. From within, I am fulfilled. Amen.

DAY 44

Delftware

For you created my inmost being;
you knit me together in my mother's womb.

PSALM 139:13

elftware is a type of earthenware in which white glaze is applied and then decorated, particularly with cobalt metal oxide, which yields the typical blue and can resist breaking at high firing temperatures.

The term *delftware* is usually used to describe any blue-and-white ceramic piece. Made in the Netherlands, authentic delftware is hand-painted by skilled artists. Delftware will be blue or white or polychrome (multicolored). Pieces range in price and quality from the elaborate, high-quality Royal Delft, to the moderate DeWit, to the distinguished screen-printed and more budget-friendly items.

I have a few cheaper pieces of delftware, and I have some authentic and higher-quality pieces too. I love each of the pieces for different reasons. But I'll be honest. Were a professional designer to come into my home, they might object to my eclectic use of blue and white.

I used to worry about how everyone might view my collection. I even hid some of my bizarre preferences in a

135

cabinet for fear of what visitors might think. But I am way past that stage in my design journey.

And I'm beyond worrying about what others think about my spiritual journey too.

What I love and what I'm good at are unique to me. God knit me together in quirky me-ness. Don't get me wrong. I am not perfect in my humanness, but I am divine in my union with Jesus. You might say, "You are doing this Jesus thing all wrong!" And I could accuse you of the same. However, we can't possibly understand where someone else is, let alone how they should be or how God is interacting with them.

Oftentimes, without even realizing it, we operate from the clouded mind space of deeming ourselves more and better or less and worse than another human being. Somehow we think that pastors or missionaries are better than construction workers. Or stay-at-home moms are better (or worse) than working moms or singles or whatever other calling someone else might have. These feelings, when combined with the heavy burden of sin focus (pointing the finger at all the wrong), release stress hormones because sin and judgment are not for us.

God calls each of us to a specific mission. That calling might be caring for children in a daycare or writing about truth in your basement or making a gorgeous spreadsheet that makes sure everyone on the team is on track. Each of those is important and neither good nor bad.

Today I would like to ask you to carefully assess how you came to be doing what you're doing. Are you finding ways to fulfill what God called you to do? If so, are you reacting offensively or defensively to others' opinions and judgments? Only you and God get to decide what you were made for. It's a decision that comes from within, not without.

When we stop and activate the heart-head with questions—"Am I thinking, creating, or receiving?"—and then take our new next step not from without but from within, we find our thoughts tuned in to God's thoughts. From this place of paying attention to our divine source of wisdom, we see more clearly what causes our worries and whether they hold value or are just a mock-up of what we think we should be.

So grab a pen or pencil. Now make a list of things you absolutely love—colors, pets, weather, food, clothes, shoes, art, people, hobbies, places. Write down what you think God has called you to do with those loves, and don't let anyone else tell you you're wrong. Hear this: my passion for delftware (or your passion for painting or walking in the woods or dancing to swing music or making spreadsheets work) is not a sin. I am not praying to my delftware. I did not steal it from my neighbor. There is no Scripture saying, "Thou shalt not collect pretty earthenware." I am not in bed toiling over how to get more delftware so I will have more than you. Do what sings to you.

Don't let others lie and tell you that life should be a drudgery of dos and don'ts. The Bible tells us that the "joy of the LORD is [our] strength" (Nehemiah 8:10). We are meant for joy. Anything else will cause us much unrest.

So where there is no harm, I choose to give thanks for the blessing.

THE FINISHING TOUCH

Jesus, I want to thank you for all the beautiful material things I enjoy. I come to you with boldness, as I grow in my newly renovated mind space. Amen.

DAY 45

Mind Makeover

N ot from without but from within. We've thought about how the outside world presses in on us and clamors to be heard over the quiet voice of God. We recognized that the process of becoming religious may have added to our confusion and tainted what we focus on. But from the quiet space we create with God, we can close off the world and go inside of ourselves with confidence and surrender to his path. We can ask for his wisdom and are assured that he will answer.

DAY 46

The Martha Washington

You know when I sit down and when I rise up;
you discern my thoughts from afar.

PSALM 139:2 ESV

I t was a shimmery navy blue, the likes of which I had never seen. Thick, embossed velvet set on a perfect blend of rustic, carved cherrywood. Not overstuffed, not under. It had a regal flare, but its comfort was unmatched, keeping my posture just right without being intrusive or bossy.

The Martha Washington–style chair had obviously been re-covered, but I paid no mind to what it might have originally looked like, for in its current coverage, it was perfect. I only knew I had to have this chair.

I checked the tag: $700.

Way out of my budget.

I wanted it. But far be it from me, a stay-at-home mom struggling to make ends meet, with four kids, on the waiting list for our first foster/adoption placement, to splurge on such a fancy-pants chair.

But I decided I would do it, and I would do it my way.

I laid it away, with three months to

pay. Fifty dollars here, another ten dollars there. I sold stuff on eBay. I babysat and took on teaching seven—yes, seven—extra aerobics classes. Teaching until I limped in order to get what I wanted.

And then one day on the way home from teaching three spin classes in a row, I noticed a sign on the vintage furniture shop's door. OUT OF BUSINESS. With only two hundred dollars left to pay off my Martha Washington chair, certainly I would be able to still get the chair, or at least get my money back. Right?

Nope. I was never able to hunt down the bankrupt owners. I never saw my five hundred dollars again.

I did drop about nine pounds. But that weight returned quickly, because no one is meant to teach three consecutive hours of high-intensity aerobics just so they can sit in an expensive chair.

Two years later, while combing an estate sale for treasures, I met up with that very same chair. I stared at it, as if we had been separated by war, finally reunited in euphoric bliss. It was literally the same chair I had pined for, nearly destroyed my joints over, in all its navy-blue wonderfulness.

It sat alone in a corner. A piece of yellow scrap paper taped to the back said FREE. I think I yelped "Mine!" like a toddler calling her place on the swing set. The woman running the sale said, "Well, okay!" After discussing the chair with her and my attempt to buy it two years before,

she explained how it came to her. Her father owned the building and had rented it to the couple who ran the antique and collectible furniture store. They had left, leaving behind all their treasures, never to be heard from again.

Sometimes the prayers of our heart seem like a shot in the dark. We want what we want when we want it. And when God doesn't deliver to our detailed expectations, we stew and stress and try to make things happen ourselves.

But I am moved to look at the Martha Washington, now covered in a velvety upholstery of cobalt and cream, and wonder, what if? What if I had asked for the chair? Prayed it would be mine instead of working for it myself? And then believed as if I'd received? Would I have had to wait two years? In any case it would have been a better story of how much Jesus loves me and loves to see me seated at the feet of trust and rest? I may never have gotten the chair, but I certainly would be five hundred dollars richer.

Fully supported in my wants and needs, what would it have been like to know, "He knows. And if it is to be, he *will* provide"? Psalm 35:27 says that God delights in our well-being.

You try it! Write some "What if wonderful!" scenarios to any troubles you are currently facing. For example, as we continue our house hunt, Jesus knows what I am up to. He knows my wants and needs.

Choosing to pray like I believe that God has wonderful things in store for me teaches my heart-head about the character of God. My prayers look like this: *God, thank you for hearing me. I am so excited to see what our new house looks like. I can hardly wait to see where all my favorite decorations will go. I am so excited to see what you will do next.*

THE FINISHING TOUCH

Jesus, I love how you love me. I love that you delight in my company and know exactly the plans you have for me. You are so fun, and I love you. Amen.

DAY 47

The Color of Faith

Faith is the substance of things hoped for,
the evidence of things not seen.

HEBREWS 11:1 KJV

Let's imagine together a lovely table in the corner of the room where you're sitting. It has gorgeous carved legs and a functional little drawer with the perfect pull. As far as color, we'll consult science a second (hang with me). According to light theory, the table absorbs all the colors of the spectrum except the color you see. Let's color that table a gorgeous flat navy blue. Blue has one of the shorter wavelengths, so it avoids absorption and is therefore the easiest color to see.

Blue is an exceptional color for interiors, especially in darker spaces, because it introduces light and color to a space. In a room with a lot of natural light, blue will make a room glow with a vibrancy. And in rooms

with minimal light, blue attracts the light that is available, making spaces still feel somewhat incandescent instead of like a dungeon.

You could intentionally decorate with blue to make a room feel lighter and more like the sky and sea.

Now let's think a little about your faith in terms of your little blue table. Your faith, the substance of things hoped for, is your personal set of beliefs. Sometimes circumstances make your faith go dark. Or religious doctrines intrude on what you know to be true and make your table feel like it's missing a foot.

The battle of the mind, the place where faith wobbles on a table with one leg too short, is the reason the cheese is falling off your cracker. Rogue faith paints dark, questioning colors across the truth of Jesus.

But Scripture is clear that wobbly, darkened faith can be remedied. Sometimes it takes counseling and the equivalent of whacking off the other three legs. But often, shoring up your faith is as simple as affixing a new foot to the shortened leg and painting the table a lovely shade of blue.

What's that look like?

First, we turn to the promises of God. Here are just a handful: We have abundant life (John 10:10). We have access to the source of love, joy, peace, patience, kindness, goodness, faithfulness, gentleness, and self-control (Galatians 5:22–23). We can find rest for our souls (Matthew 11:29).

Pick one of the promises you most want for yourself. Write it out and stick it on your bathroom mirror. Then say the promise. Declare your faith out loud while facing a mirror, and reflect that joyful blue truth of God. This is a tangible way to show the subconscious more of what you want to see in

your life. The subconscious listens to your voice and knows the thoughts in your head. While it might argue, "That couldn't be right," it can also be convinced, "Yes! Trusting Jesus is where I find rest."

Convincing ourselves of truth happens in the physical act of repetition. Instead of repeating worried thoughts to yourself, repeat your true beliefs and feelings. The more you do it, the more it sticks.

I am not suggesting that we avoid medical and or mental health options. Like I always say, "I love Jesus, and sometimes I need a prescription." What I am suggesting is that we take into account what is going on inside of us and outside of us. I am inviting you to actively participate in your own beliefs. I am suggesting that we take thoughts captive and invite them into a space that craves and reflects the light.

We must participate fully in our personal faith walk. We cannot expect it to come from outside ourselves. What works for me may be harmful or burdensome to you.

Today I'd like you to write out ten bold "I believe!" statements. What do you believe? Be precise—I am secure! I am brave! I believe God saves! Whatever you choose, tell your heart-head the facts, Jack! When you activate the heart-head with the statement *I believe*, the mind knows you are serious, because this girl says what she means.

Who's blue?

Yeah, not you.

THE FINISHING TOUCH

Jesus, I expect that my mind is changed, and I expect and am thrilled to see more change. Help me be more aware of what I am thinking and feeling. Help me to grow in my understanding of your light. Amen.

DAY 48

Faith Works and Dream Boards

*Faith without works
is dead.*

JAMES 2:26 NASB

This Savior, the One you said "Yes, Lord!" to, is the real deal.

I have experienced him. I don't say that to brag. I say it because I am compelled . . . moved, nearly beyond words, to declare that he is the real deal.

Five stars.

Yes!

Bravo!

Despite all the stresses and worries I've encountered, I've been able to note that they are not *because of* him. My son-in-law, Christian, and I have frequent, deep conversations about religion, history, and our individual faith walks. The other night at dinner he said, "Have you ever thought about the Scripture 'faith without works is dead'?" Of course I had. And having come from a background steeped in religious mishaps and tidbits of misinformation, I've heard all the debates about faith and works and what God really expects of us.

But then Christian pointed out the natural extension of the verse—faith in one's vision of a better way is dead without effort.

A popular trend right now is visualization and manifestation through the use of vision boards. I go slightly nuts over a concept or mood board for a bedroom makeover or a kitchen renovation, but I have my reservations about staring at pictures of a house in Hawaii and willing it to happen through positive vibrations.

Still, the majority of us must make an effort to get to where we want to go. Sure, you might win the lottery. Anything is possible. But if you want to be an architect at the firm where you are currently the receptionist, you are going to need to get a degree in architecture.

You can wish, hope, and hang pictures all over your house of things that remind you, "I want that." I don't want to burst your bubble—well, maybe I do—but that won't work, not even with "All things are possible" Scripture memory verses.

Faith without works is dead. Not because you don't believe Jesus's sacrifice was enough, but because faith is active. In order to experience the fruit of your work . . . you have to work. You have to go to the counselor to deal with your past. You have to apply yourself at work to get that promotion. You have to go for those daily walks to experience a health goal.

You can be mad at God that your dream house has not manifested when you had faith in him and believed as if you had received. But did you participate in the goal? Or did you sit idly by and just wait for it?

Today's message is twofold. First, yes! Ask, give

thanks, and believe as if you have received. Second, ask. Yes, ask questions. Discern and ponder. What direction can I go to advance the process? Am I thinking about the problem, creating future issues, or receiving God's wisdom and love? And am I looking at this from without or from within? When am I striving and interfering with God's plan, and when am I practicing faith and moving toward my goal?

I can't promise that staring at a vision board won't produce the funds to remodel your guest bath. Stranger things have happened. But you were designed by the great Creator to be his child and to do great things for his kingdom.

If you're facing questions—what job to take, whether to have another child, where to go to school, whether to say yes or no—wouldn't you love to know what he thinks would be best?

Ask him. Write out those big questions, and ask him. Then take the steps to go after the goal. This is another way to make him known as real to the heart-head.

Go on, ask him. He promised he will answer.

THE FINISHING TOUCH

Lord, I love to know your plans for me. I acknowledge the world and its ways seem enticing. However, I know that you have asked me to participate in my faith with works, not to earn your love but to experience more of your goodness. Open my ears, brighten my eyes, and increase my vision that my work may be of glory to your kingdom. Amen.

The Care and Keeping

Which of you, if your son asks for bread,
will give him a stone?

MATTHEW 7:9

The house was magnificent. Fourteen thousand square feet of Mediterranean excellence. Justin, bless him, had been nonstop in working on the elaborate mansion for nearly a year. It was not the largest project he had ever done, but it was the hardest.

About three months into the project, my husband's older brother

and business partner had been killed in a car accident. Between tending to his devastated mother, keeping all the balls in the air with the enormous build, and straightening out the business of losing a brother, partner, and friend, Justin was exhausted. On this day he needed an extra set of hands to scrape manufacturers' stickers off the windows so they could be washed and cleaned before closing.

The catch? The marble floors had just been installed. No one could walk on them for several days. Upon my arrival, Justin informed me that he needed my help on the second floor, which would require me to ride the scissor lift to an open window, climb out the cage, and climb through a bedroom window into the house. Certainly this was the least I could do for my weary husband.

One would hope so.

But I am a both-feet-on-the-floor kind of girl. I require a mild sedative to fly, though not because I am afraid of dying. I am ready to meet Jesus whenever. No, I am afraid of flying be-cause I just don't want to be off the ground. So my subconscious notified my conscious mind: "We don't climb into windows twenty-two feet in the air. Peace out."

My reaction was expected. Nausea, sweaty hands, shaking, blurred vision, and yes, uncontrollable crying, complete with convulsing and snot slinging. Justin held me close and told me to grab some lunch, go home, and rest.

I sat in my car and wept. I couldn't let him do the work alone. De-termined, I grabbed my gloves, bucket, X-Acto knife, and Goo Gone, chanted the Lord's Prayer, and climbed into the cage of the scissor lift.

To be honest, I spent a full hour in the cage—twenty minutes on the ground and forty minutes hovering above the luxurious courtyard com-plete with a glamorous swimming pool, full kitchen, and dance floor. And I kept saying the promises of Christ, but they were not luring me out on the ledge.

There are more traumatic experiences than heights, I know. But because of the intensity of my personal feelings, I remember clearly what I was thinking.

Do you really believe you are going to fall?

No. Not really.

Do you really believe the Scriptures you are chanting?

I want to.

Then do it. Believe what you are saying. Feel the comfort.

Belief is just lip service until you stop and choose to feel God's love and power. When we practice our faith, when we ask God for help, he always answers. Who among you would force your child to do something that shook them in terror without helping them?

Are you not the image of God?

We have Scripture for comfort. And comfort must be felt, even proven. I can tell you I am wearing comfy stretchy pants. You might agree that they look comfy. But that's all Target talk until you try them for yourself. Until you feel the comfort, you just can't know.

Today write about comfort and care. What do you know is comfortable? When was a time you asked for something but were met with less than you had hoped? Is there a chance that that comfort can still be met? What outcome would make you feel seen, heard, and know? Write about it.

Oh yeah, I climbed in the window and scraped thirty-three windows before dinner. Whatever the scary thing is you're facing, you've got it.

THE FINISHING TOUCH

Jesus, I am so grateful that you have good plans and a future for me. I know what to expect from your love. My mind is open to seeing more of you in every situation. I run to you with all my needs, and I hold on with the expectancy of a child on Christmas morning as I eagerly await your answer. I trust you. Amen.

DAY 50

Mind Makeover

Have you gone before the Lord to ask for something already pretty much thinking that you're going to have to DIY it? You end up looking like you're checking the box of what a good Christian would do rather than really trusting God. What was the outcome?

We've talked about approaching God a little differently. Instead of relying on ourselves and our good deeds to take care of things, I'm asking you to try acknowledging the Father who sees and knows you, who has good things planned for you. Give thanks for his thoughtful provision. Expect him to pat the comfy chair next to him and say, "That's my girl, and this is her chair, right next to me."

Today's breath prayer is simple: Not from without but from within.

Breathe this in and out. Think about all the provisions God has given you. Think about the good plans he has. Now tuck those into your heart, and turn away from the external world telling you what you should or shouldn't do. I think you will be delighted by the results!

SECTION SIX
Think Pink!

DAY 51

Pink Curiosity

Restore unto me the joy of thy salvation;
and uphold me with thy free spirit.

PSALM 51:12 KJV

I really do love pink for everything but my lip color (it makes me look pasty and washed out). For everything else, pink is fearless, feminine, and just plain fun. Whether it's a pop of rosy peach or a bold statement like a hot-pink front door, the person who paints with pink is making an announcement: this home is lighthearted and nurturing, and yes, "Come on in!"

If you haven't guessed it yet, I am a nosy neighbor. I like to know what's going on behind all those doors. Granted, I am too much of a recluse to really ask. But beyond guessing at my neighbors, my favorite brand of nosiness looks more like a show Justin and I watch on YouTube called *Abandoned Scotland*. Basically it's the adventures of a Scotsman, who may or may not speak English, armed with an iPhone and a GoPro strapped to his head, as he and his wife travel around the lush landscape of Scotland in search of abandoned properties.

Much like explorers of caves go spelunking as a hobby, the two wander stony remains. Sometimes they find entire castles, churches, and homesteads. They do no harm, never taking any of the treasures left behind by the displaced tenants. They snap photos of the more memorable features, then move on to the next mystery.

But one house they ventured into left me with desperate curiosity.

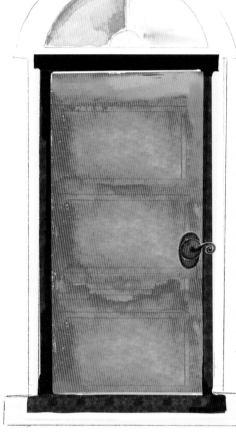

A tiny house in the middle of nowhere, untouched for what appeared to be fiftyish years. It was obviously unkempt, recognizably abandoned. They knocked on the handcrafted door and peeked in the murky windows and then, without an ounce of effort, opened the front door. The calendar on the wall read "October 1974." There were breakfast dishes in the sink, cobwebs, and rodent traces all around. On the kitchen table lay a Bible, a dehydrated and crunchy looking coffee cup next to it. A newspaper, confirming the same vacancy date as the calendar, was neatly folded in the middle of the table.

As the curious couple walked the perimeter of the outside, I wondered about the dreams that built that house. I know the lives in that house mattered. Surely somewhere on this planet someone knows what became of the visionaries who made their home in the verdant countryside a few miles west of Aberdeen.

And while we could guess—by the faded pink quilt and the piles of pastel-colored quilting squares spied in some corner—that the owners loved the mismatched and handsewn, we cannot know what they felt or how they loved or what they believed. And we certainly can't wipe away whatever it was that made them disappear.

The realization that we can't control what happens to our loved ones or how they feel is a stressor we don't like to acknowledge. When we love and care about our people, we feel more at ease when we know for sure they are safe and well.

Unfortunately, the reality is that we cannot save our families. I think somewhere inside us, we all know that. But that doesn't stop us from contriving to do things like be sure our kids have good friends and good school experiences so that they can get into the best college so they can get good jobs, get married, and ride off into the happy sunset. Further, we can't tell them how to feel when their friends gossip behind their backs or when their father is turned down for that promotion.

If I could make all that happen . . . if I had a magic wand to wave away the uncertainty and pain, I would be God and the entirety of Jesus's ministry would be for naught. And let's be honest. I would not make a good God.

That doesn't mean I shouldn't swing my pink door open and invite folks in. I can assess how to help my loved ones, answer when they knock, and let them know they are always welcome. But I do not, by my pink door or happy dreams, get to decide what anyone else does or how anyone else feels. This is a hugely important concept.

Write out "I do not get to decide how anyone else feels" on a note card or sticky note. Today as you encounter life, read it. Say this in your mind or even out loud. Note how it feels to let go of the feeling of worrying about how others feel. Do you feel the weight lift? Feels good, huh?

THE FINISHING TOUCH

Jesus, help me to remember that you know better than I. Amen.

DAY 52

Little Pink Houses

Do not be conformed to this world, but be transformed by the renewal of your mind, that by testing you may discern what is the will of God, what is good and acceptable and perfect.

ROMANS 12:2 ESV

When our newlywed time in the little blue house at the edge of town was over, I found us a pink stucco two-bedroom, one-bath rental just over the railroad tracks on Oak Street. The color, the purest and most perfect pink, was all I needed to sign on the dotted line. Justin, not so much.

On the day we moved, I learned something new, something I will never forget. The little pink house had an olive-green circa 1974 gas oven and cooktop. I had no experience with this type of appliance. So when I brought a box into the kitchen from the truck, I set the box on the stove top, unaware of this thing called a pilot light.

The short version is, we went to lunch and came home to our new pink house—filled with thick black smoke. The box had been simmering on the stove for an hour. Any longer and the lacy French-country-shabby-chic-à-la-Jami would have caught fire and the entirety of our life on Oak Street would have been abruptly moved over two blocks to the only other rental available. And it was mustard yellow.

This memory is important: I now know with my conscious mind that pilot lights exist. But it's also a lesson about the subconscious's ability to never forget.

Is it beneficial to know the pilot light is there? Yep. But there's no point in harping over the pilot light. I needn't fear or hate the house because of the pilot light. There's also no reason to avoid pilot lights. They have some benefits.

You probably know where I'm going with this. I can expect to learn from my mistakes and mishaps, but I don't expect to be ruled by them. Worrying about what could have been or will be is the nemesis to peace. But *not* stewing over our mistakes and mishaps is easier said than done. Am I right?

The mind is a powerful tool and a perfect blend of practicality and whimsy. However, it must be organized.

What parts of your mind are in a heap of fear? What do you need to identify as a real threat? What do you need to identify as helpful (like a pilot light) but not detrimental to your current well-being?

In this mind space, which will have a tendency to be cluttered, we can keep what is important without making it the center of our attention, by—you guessed it—writing it all out and then reading it out loud.

But just like we need to remove the box from the stove with a pilot light, we need to remove some of the worry clutter that simmers in our minds. Do you really need to worry about which college your kid will attend all day every day from the beginning of their junior year to the end of their senior year? Maybe schedule a day every other week to take your kid out to lunch to chat about it. Or perhaps you're worried about forgetting to put the trash out . . . again. Set a reminder on your phone.

We must have an organized brain space in each moment, or we risk getting caught in a simmering cycle of physical defeat and spiritual angst.

When you feel your anxiety creeping up, stop and ask whether it's something that is a real, immediate threat. If not, what can you do to remind yourself that it's a pilot light, but the box isn't on fire? Can you take care of it now (send that email, set up that lunch date, etc.)? Or maybe you can set up a reminder somewhere to deal with it later. Or maybe you can recruit help from an expert in the area you're concerned about (a doctor, a school counselor, a work mentor).

If there is an immediate threat that needs to be dealt with, take a deep breath and ask if you're thinking, creating, or receiving. Then tackle the problem from a place focused on God's plan.

In all this, remember that God loves you . . . completely and without abandon. If you are his child, he will not judge you for leaving the box of fears on the stove, and he won't be angry that your beautiful pink walls are a little scorched. After all, perfect love expels all fear (1 John 4:18 NLT).

THE FINISHING TOUCH

Heavenly Father, I expect to see you in the morning sunrise, in pops of magenta and blush. I expect to see you as the sun lulls low, setting into laps of creamy pink, rose gold, and peach. But help me also expect to see you as I learn from my mistakes and grow in wisdom and understanding under the protective comfort of your love. Amen.

DAY 53

Shabby Chic

*They pour new wine into new wineskins,
and both are preserved.*

MATTHEW 9:17

Shabby chic is a brand of interior design in which furniture and decor are picked for their aged appearance or the distressed aspects of their construction. Newer items are antiqued to give the appearance of wear and tear. The mixture of patterns and textures knows no bounds in this aesthetic. Shabby chic is an explosion of femininity, and gingham prints are the magic that is created with whites, creams, and faded pastel colors. Pops of the past are welcome, and hand-embroidered tea towels are a perfectly acceptable bedroom accent.

I love all things frilly and rugged. And for a long while, I berated myself for wanting more of things like this. As if wanting was materialistic and somehow sinning. But want and pleasure are part of our creation. Stifling our natural inclinations actually causes stress in the subconscious, whose main job is to keep you safe, comfortable, and surrounded by what is familiar and good for you.

Appreciating beautiful things or wanting money to buy those things is not actually a sin. A sin is something that steals and destroys. So yes, if you are shoplifting trinkets to make your room a little more chic than shabby, that's a problem. But if no harm is being done by your adoration of your great grandmother's sewing kit, and if it looks lovely on the sideboard you just distressed, then love that which you love and let it remain.

The root of all kinds of evil is loving something—like money—more than God (1 Timothy 6:10). It is when we start disobeying God's commands in pursuit of material that we need to stop and evaluate what we are feeling and why, without jumping to the judgment of self and others.

This is what I love about the practice of organizing our thoughts to test our beliefs and moving into a better space—one where Jesus is the focus. We can see where our beliefs have been thrown off-kilter.

In our culture, wealth is portrayed as wicked. The penniless person is the hero or heroine. Think about the movie *It's a Wonderful Life*. Certainly it is a touching and thought-provoking illustration of focusing on what is good and why life matters. But it's the portrayal of the banker I want you to consider. He's portrayed as greedy and needing to be fixed. What other books and movies can you think of that lure us into thinking that money is inherently evil? I could probably write a hundred books on all the lies and delusions I had about money and desire.

For much of my life, if I saw something I wanted, I felt guilt and shame. And I would write long, loopy-lettered journal entries promising to "try harder not to think about all the things I love." I would look at others who had lots of things or success or a talent I wished I had, and I would judge them for not being like me and shunning the ways of the world.

Until I met with grace. Grace is the reminder we are loved unconditionally.

Desire is part of our design because it motivates us to seek more of God. The bottom line is, we are scrambling, constantly fighting against ourselves as we are created and then judging others to justify our lack. It appears wise and godly. But not all things that appear good are good. It is all about balance. Ask yourself questions about how you use your money, time, and talents.

For example, my friend just bought a new house. It is exactly what Justin and I have been looking for. But the house never even went on the market. My friend learned about the house from a friend before anyone else.

I was jealous. I recognized it immediately. And then I took my jealous thought and made it a feel-good thought instead.

"I am so happy for Cheryl and Dan. What a fun story. What a beautiful house. I would love to have something similar with a cool story too. How fun."

And I felt every bit of that. And I mean it. Y'all don't know what a fool I am, sitting here grinning from ear to ear as I process how much fun it is to turn shabby, defeatist words into chic, blessing words. Go on—try it! See how amazing someone else is. See how good God has been to them, and know that his storehouse is overflowing with good things for you too.

THE FINISHING TOUCH

I love you, Lord. I love that you created me to love and enjoy certain things. I expect to love you most. Guide me in this wisdom. Amen.

DAY 54

Not so Fancy

*Greater love has no one than this, that someone
lay down his life for his friends.*

JOHN 15:13 ESV

Growing up, I was often confused by the messages coming at me in church.

On one side was the formal, rule-driven faith widely discussed. But then there were all these stories about this informal Jesus. Jesus wandering through a wheat field on the Sabbath, gnawing casually on a sprig. Jesus giving no rules to the thief on the cross on how to obtain paradise—just saying yes. The criminal by his side was not dunked in the river, and there is no record of his good deeds.

The means by which they died— the old rugged cross—seemed their only bond. And that is what unites us as well. Just the cross. Well, the symbol of the cross, representing the restoration of the resurrection. But even the resurrection is pretty casual. The tombstone was just rolled away, no biggie.

But it's today's Scripture that grabbed my attention and never let me look back. He

laid down his life for his *friends*. Friendship is the essence of easygoing, lighthearted living. I do not rehearse or contrive words before calling my best friend. I can say anything to her. If she has a question about my tone or belief, she just asks more questions or says, "Wait just a minute . . ." But she has never hung up on me or cast me into the bowels of hell.

That is not how friends behave.

And of my friendships, there are some that have stood the test of time. Others I have outgrown or deemed less than friendly. But Jesus has remained true and proved to have staying power despite my tantrums, doubt, and endless complaints. No greater friend have I than one who can listen to me drone on and on.

But casual intimacy has another, deeper name—unconditional love. Love without contingency. No matter how bad your breath smells or how moody and temperamental you are, you are loved. And nothing you can do can separate you from your heavenly friend.

If you're in the process of remaking your life, picking out the proverbial tile and new carpet, and you pick out a pink monstrosity of a carpet, it's okay. Jesus is there not only as your general contractor but as your friend to help you go back and make another, better choice. Unless you have both of those ideas solidly in mind, your foundation will crack under the pressure of old terrors and future unknowns, and you'll wind up in a constant state of "under construction."

We can expect Jesus to bring his peace and joy "on earth as it is in heaven" (Matthew 6:10) when we pray.

Why, then, would we expect anything less?

Expect to be dazzled by things that bring you joy, and you will see more of them. And this is not a fancy parlor trick. This is how we were made. We see more of what we focus on. Can you pick your child out of a mess of kids at the park? Of course you can. You know how they swing their right leg out when they run or how they fuss with their hair. You know their laugh and their penchant for mud puddles. You know what you love. You know who your people are. You know what you are accustomed to and what you are alerted to. So with that built-in feature, tell yourself the goodness you want to see. And then you can expect to testify to his generous, comfortably chic goodness because you have seen it with your own eyes.

This is the feeling, the comfort of friendship. Sometimes formality, especially when practiced, can make some of my suggestions seem pretty bold. Talk to Jesus like he's sitting right here? *Yes.* You want to meet with peace—make it real to the heart-head by practicing that friendship. Feel and experience his casual constancy. Right now, if he were sitting in the chair next to you . . . what do you have to say? Say it, friend! Write it all out!

What a cherished friend we have in Jesus!

THE FINISHING TOUCH
Jesus, I am so thankful you call me friend.
I love you and I like you. Amen.

Mind Makeover

Hear me when I say, I have been in the throes of a real panic attack. I am not making light of anxiety. But I am compelled to address the leaky faucet in the broken-down, filthy kitchen, the heart of the home. The drip, drip, drip that plagues us?

Worry.

Plain old worry. Not a broken-pipe explosion.

Drip, drip.

Worry dilutes the promises of Christ. And friend, it is not for us. Worry does us no good. It is time to stare down at the rickety, rotted floors beneath our feet and take back the goodness God promised us. We are able to do this because God loves us. The joy of the Lord is our strength. So what do you love? What delights you? Write it all out! Feel it. Feel the pen in your hand. Delight in the loops and swirls! And really think about what you love. This is the practice of meditating on the words of your mouth and falling in love with the God of your heart!

DAY 56

Chair Whimsy

He brought me out into a broad place; he rescued me,
because he delighted in me.

PSALM 18:19 ESV

I have been out of upholstery supplies I can access for a hot minute. The fabrics and cording I bought for this chair or that rocker have been shoved in a cabinet, saved for someday. I don't know when.

I got busy writing and painting, and frankly, I have a lot of chairs.

Here, now, with contracts for both my writing and my art, I am shocked and delighted.

Still . . . when I grow up, I want to be Wendy Conklin.

Wendy is the owner of Chair Whimsy. If you cracked my skull open, the inside would look a lot like Wendy's studio. Whimsy is a good place to start in description, but Wendy's chairs go on to be dreamy, delightful, hilarious, beautiful, feminine, nonsensical, and, like Spielberg's movies, sheer perfection.

Wendy takes antique and vintage

chairs and makes them into the most eclectic and marvelous masterpieces one could put their tushie on. Stripes, checker prints, and florals are combined with bright paint, twisty cording, and all the fancy your pants can handle.

On days when words aren't flowing, the children are banshees, and the garage door comes off its tracks again, I compose crafty emails I don't send asking Wendy if I can be her assistant.

It's here that Jesus's call to be content becomes an issue. Jesus asks you to be content/satisfied/happy with what you have. But lands, it's hard to stop the craving, the reaching, the worrying about what would happen if you were to miss your best life. I knew a girl like that once. She was never satisfied, never at peace. She was exhausted, stressed, and sad.

Even when she got her first book deal, she fretted and stressed about sales. Then when her art appeared in HomeGoods, she still worried no one would buy it. And then she grieved and worried over her kids, her marriage, and her mortgage.

When her kids were great, her marriage was rocking, and her mortgage was paid off, she worried about car parts, medical reports, grocery shopping, and frosting consumption. Then one day while scrolling through her social media, she landed upon Chair Whimsy.

What would it be like to live such a fanciful, carefree existence? To boldly coordinate red-and-white buffalo print with black, purple, and green florals and not give a nickel about who liked it or if it was right? What if instead of stressing over deadlines, paintbrushes, and numbers, she just created from the depths of her soul that which she loves?

And then what if she carried all that beautiful, cosmic delightfulness over into her motherhood and marriage?

What if . . .

The thing about trying to accomplish something is that *trying* often cuts off the flow of true creativity. When we focus on the bad, hard, or heavy stuff, we operate from a struggling mindset. However, our daily journeys, our families, careers, and trips to the grocery store are not supposed to feel like moving an entire dining room set complete with matching buffet.

But here's the thing—just like we can change the upholstery, we can fundamentally change our minds. Jesus said so. I believe him.

When we tell the subconscious vivid, whimsical stories about our true lives, we intrigue it and prompt the mind to look for more of what we love.

Take a minute and write out three things that you love about your life: your kids, the perfect little nook in your bookshelf, the coffee shop on the corner, swing music, how your coworker goes out of her way to say hello every morning. With the use of pen and paper or your out-loud voice, make the good things loom large in your life. Find the whimsy in your life, and then go take advantage of one of those good things. Crank up the music and dance, take a book off your TBR pile and enjoy it, go walk through the woods. If we make the lovely things the statement piece of our lives, we are more in tune with our Creator. This is where the big, divine, and brilliant ideas occur—and those ideas lead to the next peaceful, fulfilling, and whimsical ones.

THE FINISHING TOUCH

Lord, I take my seat next to you. I give thanks that you are my biggest fan and want me to know and experience your fullness. I can't wait to see where you will lead me next! Amen.

DAY 57

New Made Old?

Therefore, if anyone is in Christ, the new creation
has come: The old has gone, the new is here!

2 CORINTHIANS 5:17

I can get lost in renovation shows, in all the popular programs on channels such as HGTV. Given the number of DIY shows out there, I don't think I'm alone in my obsession with renovation and real estate. Recently, as I wandered a local retail shop's home decor aisles, I witnessed the impact the shows have had. The trend that interested me most was all the new knickknacks made to look old and worn. Galvanized tins that someone took a hammer to in order to make them look as if they were plucked from an antique store.

As a collector of genuine oldies but goodies, I was intrigued.

What is it about old, creepy houses made new that makes my heart flutter? What's up with my obsession to create something new out of something used? And what is my fascination with authentically rusty coffee cans filled with wildflowers?

The answer came to me at 3:00 a.m., as per usual.

Restoration and growth are my passion. Restoration and freedom in Jesus? Well, that is the entirety of my existence. I love to see God take someone others might regard as broken or ugly and make that person into beautiful artwork. I am obsessed with the transformation that comes when I witness someone fall into the authentic joy of grace. That is my favorite.

In home decor, "made to look old" is a great aesthetic. But in life, new in Christ means the old is gone. When we speak the opposite, when we define ourselves as broken, we simply are not speaking truth.

Dear one, we are no longer defined by sin. But when we speak the words and feel the emotions of "but I'm broken" instead of "Wow! I can't believe my eyes. I am a new creation in Jesus!," we are effectively teaching the mind that the promises of Christ are confusing.

Shoog, there is no "but" in a perfect "I love you."

God doesn't just shine us up a little and put us on display like a coffee can with daisies in it. He takes the raw materials of our talents and gifts and completely reworks us into gorgeous pieces of found artwork.

Perfect love has no faux finish. It is slow to anger, rich in mercy, and without condition. Our culturally approved professions are only lip service that pale in comparison to what is actually available to us. But what we *believe* about ourselves, what we continue to repeat in unison, often in song, surrounded by friends and family, directly affects what we receive.

No, not in the ways of material things. In the ways of peace, patience, goodness, kindness, love, in abundance. And if the words we speak are not the truth of who God is, the peace he promised is a knockoff of the original.

There's an easy fix. Don't settle for the replica. Don't fixate on the illusion. Look deep inside yourself, focus on who he says you are.

Today look up a few verses about who God says you are. Read them out loud to yourself. Not sure where to start? Try Isaiah 43:4; Song of Songs 4:7; Romans 8:1, 38–39; Galatians 4:7; Ephesians 2:4–5; and 1 Peter 2:9–10.

Just in case you miss it, I'll give you a hint.

You are an authentic treasure, the real deal.

THE FINISHING TOUCH

Jesus, I want to see more of your authentic self! In knowing the real you, I will experience more freedom in the real me! Amen.

DAY 58

Boho Beachy

I will give thanks to you, LORD, with all my heart;
I will tell of all your wonderful deeds.

PSALM 9:1

W e're currently looking for a house on the same lake my parents live on. In an effort to align my mind and my subconscious with experience (still looking for our new house and, nope, haven't found it yet), I have made a few small purchases.

Those purchases include a hot-pink "Lake Life Is the Life" throw pillow and a sign that reads "Lake Life Living." Obviously there is a definitive line between my saying "I have a house on Lake Conroe" and the statement "We would like to buy a house on Lake Conroe," but we know owning a home on the lake is feasible for us.

Though it has been a long search, and a lot of what we thought we wanted originally and what we now would like to have has changed, my subconscious is on alert to the reality of the possibilities.

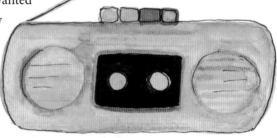

Let's settle in a minute and dream about coastal design and its bright, reflective colors. Whites, blues, crispy pastels, and the colors of a sunset communicate the spirit of celebration, vacation, and beach party. Simplicity is key in a true coastal renovation. You don't want to dust four hundred cluttered shelves. You want to lay in the sand, bask in the sun, and frolic in the waves. A basic rule of color in coastal design is "sand, sea, sky."

Of course, coastal design can also include broad muted stripes, the hues and serenity of sea glass, and the bumpy texture of seashells and pink coral. Not to be confused with nautical-themed decor—which uses red, white, and blue with collections of sailboats, anchors, and fish—a coastal vibe embraces the outside without making a kitschy tribute to the local gift shop or crab shack.

Now think about combining that coastal dreaminess with bohemian or boho decor. Boho is a colorful, eclectic look adored by many that often evokes a beachy vibe with its natural light, wicker baskets, refurbished chairs, sideboards, and botanicals. The walls of a good boho-styled space are light. They are either the softest of white or cream, pale gray, or barely visible blues, pinks, peaches, or sage. If you have a "Wanderlust" bumper sticker on your baby-pink 1962 VW bus or are a free-spirited junk-store junkie, boho may be your vibe. Bohemian style features an unfiltered mix of furniture styles, patterns and colors, and imaginative ornamentation with an asymmetrical flow. Boho design is most often extremely casual and effortless, with a relaxed hippie-vibe approach.

Are you dreaming with me yet?

Do you feel the smile on your face?

This is the feeling we're meant to enjoy. God created all this good stuff for us to celebrate and *expects* us to love it as much as he does. So let's create some positive nods to your hopes and goals. Collect some things that you love, that make you feel good or remind you of God's goodness, and display them for you to see every day. Even a tiny shelf or tabletop is a great way to further increase your faith, to remind you of the blessings God has for you no matter where you are currently in your life. Much like the ease of the coastal vibe, the simple act of investing in a portion of your end goal envelops you in the journey. It gives you something tactile to hold on to as you keep moving forward in faith that God has the best in mind for you.

To calm your mind and lift your spirit, you might use Pinterest images or a polaroid of the porch swing from the Airbnb you visited in Cape Cod. A great technique is to close your eyes and imagine yourself in one of these peaceful places. What do you hear, feel, see? Settle in there and let your body relax. Whether you are destined to have wide-plank wooden floors that reach out to your deck overlooking the lake or you just feel better when contemplating this aesthetic, much of our stresses are simply feelings we need to swap out for better feelings.

Choose to believe that God is good even if you don't get the house of your dreams.

THE FINISHING TOUCH

Jesus, open my eyes to more of what good is to come. Alert me to sand, sea, and sun, where I can experience your easy yoke and burden-free way. Amen.

DAY 59

Warm Thanks

*But thanks be to God! He gives us the victory
through our Lord Jesus Christ.*

1 CORINTHIANS 15:57

E veryone knows that an unfinished basement is cold, drafty, and not exactly the height of fashionable decor. And if you open the doors of that basement and invite in the winter chill, you might eventually find enough blankets to get used to it, but it will never be comfortable. It's the last place you would take a visitor to make them (or you) feel comfy and welcome.

Our heart-heads are rather the same. Why do we allow them to blow icy-cold terrors through our peace for no real life-threatening reason?

I can tell you, but you might not like the answer.

Worry and stress, whether bone-chilling or run-of-the-mill, when experienced for an extended period of time, become significantly important to the heart-head. Because you have experienced the feelings of your stress, the mind has marked that stress *of value*. Even though you try to put it away, insulate it, and leave it in the attic, those feelings made a frosty mark on you.

While we need stress hormones to help us escape the clutches of a hungry black bear, we don't need them for every crafty news report, enraged Facebook rant, or note home from the teacher. In this day and age, we are overstimulated and lacking rest. However, over the course of this devotional, your conscious mind has been made privy to the subconscious mind's hoarder habits. Now when that stress memory finds its way out of the storage unit and back into your life, you can use the conscious mind to put it back and close the windows on the frosty air. Save the subconscious's reaction for lunch with your less-than-pleasant mother-in-law or your camping trip to Yosemite, where the bears are real and you need to be ready to run.

But we are promised more than just a mind free of full-on winter storms. Our minds can be changed into the warm and cozy safety we were promised. Like I said on day 56, Jesus said so—I believe him.

But I have learned to believe him through being aware of his presence and giving thanks for it. How? Let's think about it in terms of how you might decorate for warmth and comfort.

While visitors to your home might miss the details and intricacies, and sometimes we put random pieces here or there just to fill space, the intentional displaying of objects you love (like the toile fabric chair that reminds you of France or the porcelain teacups your grandmother gave you) adds warmth to a room.

In interior design we add warmth with color and texture or soft lighting and fire. Heavy patterns and weaves, along with richly stained woods, terra-cotta, browns, and golds, create a cozy feel. Add a heavily braided wool rug to a bare concrete stained floor and tuck an overstuffed velvet chair in the corner guarded by loosely tied baskets filled with sprigs of cotton stems and cattails, and you just went from cold to cozy Rocky Mountain getaway.

Wouldn't you love to have this cozy comfort in your heart-head too? Well, my friend, you can find Rocky Mountain cozy in the practice of giving thanks. Sincere, heavily felt offerings of gratitude add warmth and depth to the intimacy between the giver and the receiver. You can feel the difference. A teenager headed out the door to practice might chirp "Thanks!" over his shoulder in reference to the peanut butter crackers you tossed at him. When the mom across the street who brought you flowers and wanted to say thank you for saving their dog and calling 911 before their house was a pile of ash, she means that from the depths of her soul.

So yes, shut the windows on practicing worry. But then fill your heart-head with the warmth of deep-rooted, real thanksgiving. What's one big-time event you're thankful for? Set up something to remind you about how God came through. Maybe it's a stone with a word on it sitting on your mantel, a photo hung on your wall, or a necklace that reminds you of a time and place. Whatever it is, let it warm you up and snuggle inside God's graciousness.

THE FINISHING TOUCH

Father, I want to raise the warmth of my voice and the songs in my heart. I am so grateful and happy you hear me. You know my heart. Thank you for answering. Amen.

Mind Makeover

We've talked more about creating good feelings and beliefs to replace the old beliefs. This section was fun for me because I discussed things I love. Love is a feeling. And while we have plastered it on T-shirts and hung our "Live, Laugh, Love!" signage, the feelings of the past, the disappointments, and the clutter in our minds can keep us from experiencing the feelings of being seen, heard, and known.

I would like to invite you to take a look at what you love. What brings you pleasure and comfort? Is it a certain food? A scent? Or a particular home decor? Is there a space in your life that motivates you? Consider the feelings you have when you are living in the moment, noticing the sunset or hearing a bird chirp. When is the last time you laughed? Or felt goose bumps over an amazing story? When we note these feelings and then attach the feelings of gratitude to them while incorporating the promises of Jesus, we are intentionally changing our minds! What an easy assignment.

Let us practice out loud. "I love . . ."

SECTION SEVEN
The Greens

Green with Envy

*A heart at peace gives life to the body,
but envy rots the bones.*

PROVERBS 14:30

Green is one of my favorite colors in both nature and art (shocking, I know). In design, green is a nod to nature, a not-so-subtle tribute to leaves, trees, brush, and lush grass. A dark-green front door indicates wealth and prestige. A lime-green front door probably opens to the beach or lakefront and matches against with sand, sea, surf, and your sun lounger. A sage-green front door means the homeowner is serene, peaceful, and a lover of nature.

Perhaps green home decor lost its trendiness with the passage of avocado shades, once proudly displayed in pleather sofas, polyester curtains, stoves, toasters, and wall phones in the sixties and seventies. Or the hunter greens of the eighties—a nod to country-club living—seen in the smooth, rich lines of embossed wallpapers, with dashing foxes and hounds, and heavy drapes in potent plaids.

Unfortunately, green is also closely associated with jealousy.

"Green with envy" means you have so much covetousness, you are on the brink of vomiting and could use a big dose of Dramamine. But this can invoke further stomach upset because we worry about the fact that we are coveting. We have been taught wanting is wrong or sinful (see day 53).

Then many of us find ourselves on our sofa watching renovation shows and beach house–hunting programs and are left feeling "green," wanting something that belongs to someone else and deeming ourselves *awful*.

But wanting something is different from coveting something. Wanting is looking at something and appreciating it enough to say, "Someday I'd love to have something like that." Coveting takes it to a whole other level: "I want that thing. I want it now, and I will do anything to get it."

When my husband sees a green John Deere tractor or other piece of masculine, testosterone-producing construction or farm equipment, he always says, "I wish I had that and that that guy had one just like it!"

I find this an intriguing way of stating a want without begrudging the owner in possession of said thing. See the difference?

This distinction has been a big help to me as far as stress and worry go. Want and admiration are part of our design. We progress in work and

wisdom when we are motivated to acquire things that benefit us and our families.

This is a simple trade—work for a wage to pay for things. It isn't until we allow our want to morph into judgment, hate, or jealousy for another individual that we become an ugly green color.

Here's the good news: we are able to redirect our minds from the ugliness of coveting by simply stating the facts. "Oh! I just love her new sofa!" And then we wish that person well, either in our minds or in person. We refuse to allow the item we are in awe of to become an idol or pursuit that distracts from the truth of who we are in Christ.

Think for a second about something you've seen that you'd really like to have: the vacation to Mexico your neighbor took, the funky chair you saw online, a healthy body like your sister. Now think about how awesome that thing is for your neighbor, friend, or family member.

Give praise for it for them. Now pray, asking God what might take you in the direction of that lovely thing. Would that pursuit bring you closer to God? If so, what is a step you can take today to start the journey? Thank God for the provisions he's given you, and release your guilt over appreciating the good things in life.

THE FINISHING TOUCH

Jesus, I love and expect to spy an abundance of green all around me. Every leaf, every blade of grass is a nod to your perfect design. My senses are alive with the sound of abundance and gratitude for everything you have created. It's my heart's joy to give you thanks! Amen.

DAY 62

His Will

Rejoice always, pray continually, give thanks in all circumstances; for this is God's will for you in Christ Jesus.

1 Thessalonians 5:16–18

I n 2013 we were a family of seven. In an effort to adopt a sibling group, we moved from a house we owned outright to a four-thousand-square-foot rental. The rent payment was not something we were accustomed to.

No mortgage is a blast, but our convictions and desire to help these young sisters trumped our budget fears, so we moved. A month after we scrambled to set up our new home, the little girls were moved to the home of their distant relative. The collapse of what had seemed like God's will for our family left me baffled and, frankly, hurt. I'd truly believed I had moved in the direction he would be pleased with.

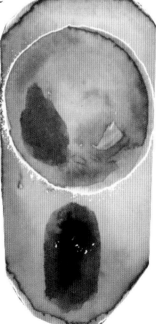

I admit I delighted in decorating the traditional-style home, with big white pillars in the front, deep-red brick, a glossy evergreen door, and white crown molding. The house was like nothing we had lived in before. Granted, it was a little more cookie-cutter than the homes we designed and built, but it was also about twelve hundred square feet larger than any home I had ever lived in.

With everyone in their own rooms for the first time in their young lives, I decided that instead of stressing over what I believed was a wrong message from the divine, I embraced the space and made it home, and I took on the mindset of practicing gratitude.

When I wondered why we were in a neighborhood in the middle of town instead of the dream home we had built on our ranch, I gave thanks for a new adventure, a change of decor, and the ease of living in the city. When I grieved the placement of the girls in a different home, I gave thanks that he promised to make all things right and new.

It wasn't until I found gratitude in my failed plans that we received a call in the middle of the night asking us to welcome a baby boy into our home as a foster placement. A placement that would make us a family of eight, with plenty of room for him to stay and eventually be adopted by us. Something that would not have happened in the house on the ranch or if the sibling pair of sisters had been placed with us.

For this, I am forever grateful.

It is this that I hold most dear: God knows the plans he has for us, plans to prosper, not harm us; plans for a hope and a future (Jeremiah 29:11). Now that is every reason to give thanks!

Today I think it would be nice to write out a situation from your past that now makes so much sense to you. When you have finished, jot some notes to self and answer this question: What word or phrase from this experience is my reminder that God knows the plans he has for me?

I'll go first: Charlie.

THE FINISHING TOUCH

Thank you, God, for your good and pleasing will. Thank you for never leaving me. If and when I have moved in a direction other than the one you would have me choose, I rest easy, knowing I cannot be separated from you and that even a wrong choice can be made right. Amen.

Did I Say Thank You?

God has surely listened
and has heard my prayer.

PSALM 66:19

Living on my parents' second story while house hunting has made editing a book about stress-free living . . . challenging. I am getting to practice what I believe. And gratitude doesn't go out of style.

So in the midst of a massive moment of frustration, I listed some things I am grateful for. I was hard-pressed. My mom was yelling up the stairs, "Come check and see if you can see my underwear through these dress slacks!"

But then I remembered a time when Justin and I believed we were in so deep, there was no way out. We were finishing a custom home. The clients, who initially were a delight, had morphed into an incubus. They changed their minds more often than they made them up. Their demands and over-the-top changes wore on the budget and our nerves. But it was on the final day, the finish line, that everything came to a terrifying halt.

Justin called me from his truck. I had been expecting his call, as the city inspector had been doing the final inspection on the home. I knew by the tone of Justin's voice that it was bad. According to the inspector, the entire house was seven inches over the property line. The neighbor, an unhappy fella, would have to be informed, and we would need to ask him to sell us the appropriate border before we could close and be done with these clients. There would be no telling what he would demand as compensation for encroaching on his property. Worse, he could just refuse and demand that we get the house off his land.

I don't remember much about the forty-five minutes that followed. I cried. Don't tell, but I am pretty sure Justin did too. The new homeowners made it clear they would not be buying the house and that they would be in touch with their lawyer. We had just built our own home and closed the month before. Our home, our savings, and our future hung in the balance.

I fell to my knees and begged God to help us. I stayed there and waited for more news.

When Justin finally called back . . . it had all been a *mistake*.

The inspector had used an old survey. The house was perfectly placed in the middle of the lot, just as Justin had carefully planned at the beginning of construction.

Later I realized that I didn't remember giving thanks, certainly not as fervently as I had begged for help. However, you can bet I gave thanks as soon as God revealed the news to me (and many times afterward too).

See, there is no bad time for gratitude. But often it's best practiced in the now. Thanking God is acknowledging his evergreen and eternal provisions. It helps anchor our minds in peaceful places. Often we are thinking about the future. You can be reading this, and your mind might be an hour ahead, wondering if you'll beat traffic or have time to stop for coffee.

When it comes to financial stresses, we are habitually in such anguish with worry, we only think about the worst-case scenarios that might make us wither up and die. Rest assured, those disasters don't exist yet. They are not happening as you read.

Only now, this minute, is your concern. We can shut down the production of stress hormones and give the heart-head some proof of God's provision when we assess what is happening right this second. What do you need at the moment? What would make you feel seen, heard, and known? What is around you that you are grateful for?

For example, right this second I have my ice water to my left, in my favorite cup. My diffuser is humming and spewing eucalyptus and violet. The temperature is just right, and my UGGs are toasty on my feet. I have everything I need right now. Praise God!

If you're too overwhelmed to focus on the now, think about when you've experienced his provision in the past. Once your mind is a bit settled, look around you again. What are you thankful for in the moment? Write down some of the things you're grateful for so you can use the list to anchor yourself another time. Recounting the good shows the mind more of what you want to see. And yep, that is science (see day 37). More good news is coming!

THE FINISHING TOUCH

Jesus, thank you for all the times you have shown up and saved me. I want to thank you for every single moment, especially the ones that I forgot about. You are so good. I am so grateful that you call me friend. Amen.

DAY 64

Fall in Love with Gratitude

They are like trees planted along the riverbank, bearing fruit each season. Their leaves never wither, and they prosper in all they do.

PSALM 1:3 NLT

As the season of fall rolls around every year, pops of crunchy retired leaves, fat pumpkins, and fancy gourds burst forth. At least in some places. My Texan sisters and I don't really get autumn. We want to. We dream of sweaters and mugs of pumpkin spice lattes, but unless we have visited Vermont in October, we are just pining over a Hallmark movie and the illusion of a crisp fall night.

In Texas the seasons don't feel like spring, summer, fall, or winter. It is more like summer, summer, summer, maybe winter, and oh, it's freezing! And then we swim and grill hot dogs the next day. Recently Justin needed a new battery for his truck. The clerk at the auto parts store said, "Yeah, I've been selling a lot of batteries since this cold spell hit."

It was sixty-eight degrees.

Still, I set the resin pumpkins and apple pie candles in the foyer and line the table with silky fall botanicals. Certain seasons in our culture require some bling.

While the leaves on the elm tree in our side yard give up the ghost the second it drops below ninety degrees, other plants and trees pay no mind to weather and are unaffected by the seasons.

We live on the edge of Sam Houston National Forest. The evergreens are true to their nature and soar so high, one might think they are tickling the clouds. But the greatest testament to evergreen survivability is the sago palm. Sagos look like miniature palm trees. With feathery fronds, pineapple-textured trunks, and roots going back to prehistoric dates, the plant has some grit and grace. We have seven sagos in our North Houston yard. In February 2021 Houston was hit with a nasty freeze. Yeah, yeah, I know, Michigan—you experience this daily. But I raise your minus-10 degree winters and ask you how you would fare in 110 degrees with 250 percent humidity.

All right then. After four days with no electricity or water, we barely glanced at our frozen sagos. But when the lights, water, and temperatures returned to normal, we were pretty confident the palmy yard decor would have to be dug up and replaced with something new. This would be a big deal. One of the would-be casualties was nearly four feet tall and sat nicely in a picturesque corner of our yard. But it was a neighbor who told us, "You can't kill those. Just cut the tops off—they'll be fine."

Hardly trusting him but having to follow his advice since he was sitting on his front porch watching us, we did as he prescribed. Sure as Texas sweet tea goes with summer sunsets, the seven sagos rejuvenated and are thriving in all their luxurious green color. You can't keep a good sago down. For this, there is a season to give thanks. And that season is every single day.

God created us to be flourishing trees planted by streams of water (Psalm 1:3). With every situation we can be made stronger, more resilient, and ready to be brought into the glory of our redemption.

Take a second to read these truths out loud to yourself: You are the beloved. You are the tenacious go-getter Jesus knew you would be. Yes, there are harsh seasons and sometimes the tops need to be cut off to allow for growth. But every day, in every way, you are seen, heard, and known.

Now give thanks, knowing that gratitude is year-round evergreen decor. And all the ferns and ficuses say, "Thank you and amen."

THE FINISHING TOUCH

Jesus, I was created for worship and gratitude. I am so thankful for my creation. Thank you, for I am resilient and strong. Amen.

Mind Makeover

Shifting to a mindset of gratitude is where we meet with our true feelings about abundance. We are promised abundance in Scripture. That may look like deep friendships or beautiful landscapes. And it may be an abundance of deep gratitude for what we're learning in hard times. And having much may even translate into financial overflow. Here's the thing—abundance, in whatever form, is something to be thankful for. Don't let teachings (such as years of wealthy movie villains) make you nervous about being grateful for the green stuff or any material thing you love.

God gives good things, and we are able to use those things appropriately when grounded in our appreciation and thanksgiving in any moment. Focusing on what is right in this moment, thanking God for whatever amount is in our checking accounts, praising him for the food on our tables and the socks on our feet . . . these things teach the heart-head something new about God's goodness and the truth about the unknowns. Take time today to look for the good, the evergreen, the blades of grass and the blazes of sunshine on your face. And . . . give thanks.

DAY 66

The Rocking Chair

I no longer call you servants, because a servant does not know his master's business. Instead, I have called you friends, for everything that I learned from my Father I have made known to you.

JOHN 15:15

I know that this book should probably have my husband's name, Justin, right next to mine on the cover. What can I say? I would not know much of anything about construction and renovation if it weren't for the years of being his wife and friend. I hate to tattle on him, but I promise there are enough accolades to balance out this one lapse in gift-giving judgment: for our first Christmas together, he bought me a *Betty Crocker* cookbook and an *apron*.

Knowing him as I now do, I know this gift had the most genuine of meanings. I know when he bought the cookbook that he intended it as a reference to the beautiful meals we make together. I don't want to talk about the apron.

But let me tell you, he more than redeemed himself on our third Christmas together. I was pregnant with Maggie. Our purse strings were double knotted. On Christmas morning he asked me to sit on

195

the couch and wait for him. He stepped out onto the front porch of our little pink house on Oak Street. When he came back inside, he was carrying a beautiful, hand-carved maple rocking chair. Justin had purchased the heirloom for me in celebration and hopeful expectation of our first child. But wait

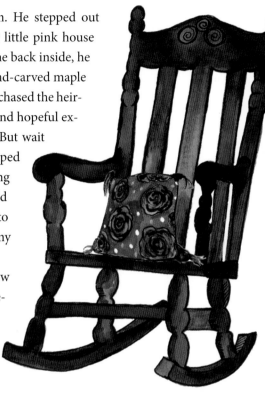

. . . it gets better. Neatly wrapped under the tree—in wrapping he had at his shop that would grace my packages for years to come—was a collection of my favorite childhood books.

Justin is a man of few words, but he wrote something inside the cover of one of the books. "Merry Christmas 1994. I like you. Justin."

I like you.

Since that time, we say this regularly. Actually, we say, "I love you and I like you." Once, our daughter asked, "Why do you say you like me? Don't you love me?" And Justin said, "Of course I love you. You are my daughter. But I like who you are, and I enjoy your company."

Back off, ladies. He's mine.

To be liked, to enjoy the company of someone, this is a vision of our God. *He likes us* (Psalm 149:4). And he gives the absolute best gifts. In fact, he so wanted to enjoy your company that he came to earth to die a criminal's death so that you might be joined with him as friend.

Who doesn't need a good friend? Someone who likes us?

Sometimes we love by default. Our people are our people, and we profess and express love. Others of our people are more than just a random cosmic drop of the genetic hat. They are people we truly like and want to be around.

What a stress relief! You are liked by the creator of the platypus and the stars! He just loves being around you and calls you friend. Today let's think about what makes a good friend. Google it if you're not sure. Think about ways God is a good friend to you. How might you enjoy God today?

THE FINISHING TOUCH

Jesus, I like you too. I acknowledge your friendship. I give thanks that nothing can separate me from that companionship. I expect to feel you near and wait in joyful anticipation for our time together. Amen.

DAY 67

The Power of Three

Though one may be overpowered, two can defend themselves.
A cord of three strands is not quickly broken.

ECCLESIASTES 4:12

In design, odd numbers are a rule of thumb for keeping good balance, depth, and texture. While two is plenty in marriage and chess, the rule or guideline of three in home decor is simply the understanding that collections of accessories or art pair better in odd-numbered sets of three, five, seven, nine . . .

For example, let's say you have a side chair and table. The table is about twenty-nine inches in diameter. By placing three items on the table, such as a tall crystal vase with some (say three) roses in it, a heavily

textured brass frame with a picture of your kids, about half the height of the vase, and a small wooden clock, you have created an intentional, balanced seating area.

However, there are times where the rule doesn't hold. The six infant portraits I have lined on my wall is a perfectly balanced reflection of my life. I am not having another child just to have an odd number of portraits on that wall.

But this trying-too-hard-for-perfection is often what happens in our religious lives. We accept rules or laws and blindly categorize them as things we are good at or things we are bad at.

Good thing for us, God gifted us places in our spiritual walk where the power of three works to our benefit. Scripture says where two or more are gathered, Jesus is there with us. And we have the trusted help of not just the Father and not just the Son, but also the Holy Spirit.

It's that latter one (the great helper, the Holy Spirit) that is a huge benefit to us as we uncover harmful old habits and beliefs and renovate our minds with new ways to experience life. I confess I do not call on the Holy Spirit as often as I can. (I don't say *should*. Shoulds are for the law-bound. In life and in decor and design, shoulds only lead to rebellion and discord.) But there is a reason God asks us to call on the Holy Spirit for help.

The Holy Spirit is the One that brings all the juicy, mind-nourishing gifts—love, joy, peace, patience, kindness, goodness, and self-control. Our spirits know we were created for all that fruit. But when we are drowning in stress chemicals, worry, and envy, it is harder to decipher his voice. This is when we invoke the greatest helper.

Make no mistake. The Holy Spirit will show up—sometimes he'll appear in the form of the voice of a friend or counselor, or he might show up in the green leaves on the tree outside your window, or he might just help in the form of that bottle of antianxiety meds.

Let the Holy Spirit be the object of our gratitude today. Great thanks for the gift of the power of three. Amen, amen, and amen.

What does the power of three mean to you? Do you invoke the power of the Holy Spirit? And not in a churchy, impress-the-neighbors way. Alone, in the stillness, are you intentionally searching out the experience of the Holy Spirit? Do you spend time in Scripture? If you have church or religious trauma, don't call it quiet time. Instead take a few minutes today to think of a new name for this practice, and then do it.

I am thankful Jesus knows me. He is cool with me and my quirks just like he's down with whatever you relate to as well. Write out three things that are burdensome to you at this time. After that, write, "Thank you for your help with this, Holy Spirit." Now sit and feel the comfort of having handed over your worries to the One whose help you can count on.

THE FINISHING TOUCH

Heavenly Father, beloved Son, and loyal Holy Spirit, my help comes from you. I am so grateful for your love and companionship. While the world argues against odds, and balance is assumed in pairs of two and four, I know that the Three who know and love me are all I need to live a life of abundant rest on Easy Street. Thank you. Amen.

DAY 68

Craft and Mission

For we are co-workers in God's service;
you are God's field, God's building.

1 CORINTHIANS 3:9

Craftsman furniture and mission-style furniture are often mistaken as one and the same. Both have effortless wood arrangements. However, their production sets them apart. Craftsman style is grounded in the uniqueness of hand craftsmanship. Mission style is mass-produced. They have similarities in appearance, but the unique markings of the individual carpenter, joiner, or cabinetmaker are what separate the craft from man from the craft from machine.

Isn't this an interesting division? Both are lovely. However, when we look closely, the difference between manufactured versus handcrafted is apparent. Where machines methodically spit out identical pieces, the wonderfulness of individual human talent, thought, and methodology cannot precisely be re-created. A twist of a carving tool one way or the other produces varying intricacies. A particular whorl of grain in the wood can make for stunning results.

Oh, but we do love our consistencies and customs. And yet how bland and boring would life be if every detail was mass-produced?

Instead the capable hands of our Creator neatly craft each detail of our lives like a piece of Craftsman-style furniture. Yes, the carving tool God uses for you might be different from the one he uses for me, but there is a purpose behind the choice.

In a world of reproductions and mass productions, to be set apart as a delightful, purposeful, one-of-a-kind production is a special place to be.

I have a favorite quote by famed French Enlightenment author, historian, humorist, and philosopher Voltaire: "God made us in his image and we returned the favor."[9] Voltaire was renowned for his wit and often spoke of his intolerance for religious dogma, the heavy rule of the Catholic church, and the French establishments of his time. While some of his rants are way off from where we find rest, this quote remains a favorite of mine.

We are created in God's image. But then we manufacture a mass-produced God, something consistent and predictable, insisting that we know best as we add to the completed work of the cross and resurrection.

Our desperate attempts to shape our lives, or to create a reproducible pattern in plans, allows religion to rule where the Spirit would joyfully guide and nurture, direct and protect, and ultimately love us into a place of peace and freedom.

When we remove law and religion and ignore what the world tells us, we allow Jesus his proper place. And that opens the way for authentic relationships and goodness.

I can already hear some folks argue, "That's a license to do as we please. Chaos will ensue. Society will morph Jesus into whomever they wish."

Okay. Society is going to do what it's going to do with or without religion's rules.

You are not society. You are an individual, one-of-a-kind design. The Spirit will never lead you to settle, deceive, or fail. All that he asks is that we believe he'll do what's best for us and then keep in touch with him.

This place, the mind space of understanding and accepting unbridled grace, is where we are joined with Christ in the exclusive and thrilling space of expectation. No, we may not be privy to the perfected end result.

But we are assured that his will for us is goodness and mercy. And that will is perfectly crafted for you, today, right where you are.

The worries of tomorrow or the next day or the next are put at ease in the hands of such a skilled Craftsman. We can expect the outcome will be unrepeatable in the solitary and intentional design he has in mind . . . just for you.

What makes you feel unique? What makes you feel seen, heard, and known? What do you need from God? And how can you acknowledge his knowing of you and in turn experience more of his real character? Oh. It is so specific and intentionally just for you. Write it, love!

THE FINISHING TOUCH

Jesus, I have picked apart my lack and grappled with understanding. And all along you knew me and you continue to know me. As I focus on you who makes all things new, I am making easy strides that will bear much fruit and bring more of heaven to earth. In your precious and holy name. Amen.

The Mansion on the Thirteenth Green

Where there is no wood, the fire goes out;
and where there is no talebearer, strife ceases.

PROVERBS 26:20 NKJV

Two months before we packed up to move from West Texas closer to my parents, siblings, and an international airport for my speaking opportunities, we put our second oldest child, John, on a bus for marine boot camp.

Days after that, our foster love, a baby girl who had been in our home for two years, was returned to her restored mama. Bittersweet doesn't really convey the emotion we felt then—it was more like, bitter, heartbroken, and crushed with a slightly sweet aftertaste. Kind of like when you have to use your child's Bubble Fruit Magic toothpaste. It isn't going to kill you, but it's no picnic either.

The house we moved into was a loaner. A friend of my dad's had purchased it as an investment, and the property manager was trying to sell it. We agreed to show it while we stayed there and to keep it safe until it sold or we found something else. The twelve-thousand-square-foot 1970ish house was everything I love about midcentury-modern design. Soaring ceilings, thick crown molding, enormous windows, and heavy oak cabinets added a warmth to the home that made me giddy.

The house, which we'd already been told had issues, turned out to have one problem that was completely out of our control—the house had a bad reputation. One day while we were sitting on the back porch, we overheard two golfers talking about the house.

The first golfer said, "Wow! That house is huge. Look at all the stone and woodwork. Look at that sunroom. The wood detail is amazing." To which his companion said, "Yeah, I have heard it's for sale. It sat there vacant for thirty years. It was built by a professional basketball coach in the seventies. He bought it as a party house—it doesn't have a kitchen, and there are in-ground hot tubs in every room."

Actually, it had *two* full-size gourmet kitchens. It had been on the market only a couple of years. It was built by some famous coach, and he did use it for parties, but after that it was someone's regular home for many years, at which time they got rid of the one—*singular*—hot tub. But rumor and gossip had taken their toll, and we never showed the house to a single potential buyer.

Gossip (talking behind someone's back) and rumor (spreading incorrect information) do tangible damage, and not just to the person being spoken about. Gossip actually does more harm to the people doing the gossip. Scripture tells us, "Do not judge, or you too will be judged" (Matthew 7:1). For years I believed that God would exact this judgment on me. But now, in the comfort and protection of grace, I know that Scripture means something entirely different. When we judge others, we are simultaneously judging ourselves.

How? Consider this: If I think someone has an ugly house, what is it saying about my measurement of ugly? Do I think my house is prettier? Am I thinking that their house might actually be prettier than mine? Aha. See? "Do not judge, or you too will be judged" isn't a warning—it is a fact. The only way to not judge others is to evaluate only the self.

Furthermore, when we speak against someone, the person we are speaking to ends up judging us *and* the person we're tattling on. All the subconsciouses involved store the memories away, noting that none of the parties involved can be trusted. And that doesn't feel peaceable either, because, yeah, you've just been judged. Now there could be gossip about how judgmental you are. Oh my goodness.

Today plan your escape from the rumors, idle talk, and judgmental babble by writing out ten DIY escape responses.

For example, if a friend says, "Colleen is getting married. This is like her fifth husband." Society says I need to respond. Habit and casual conversation might rehash all Colleen's rehearsal dinners. But Jesus says judge not, and I know there is a proverb about gossip (see Proverbs 16:28).

What are some healthy, peaceable responses? How can I redirect this conversation? Do I need to remove myself? How can I do that politely?

Now write it out so you have a visual and physical, teachable route to more peace.

Good girl. Now, go soak in the hot tub.

THE FINISHING TOUCH

Lord God, I acknowledge and give thanks for your wisdom. I trust you. I am coming to see where I have invited worries and troubles not meant for me through how I speak. Thank you for this new way of thinking and understanding about the detriment of idle talk and gossip. I expect to be more aware of words that are not for me. Amen.

Mind Makeover

As gratitude becomes a habit and the mind sinks into the calm serenity of the evergreen peace God promises, envy, greed, and selfishness fall away from us. I would like to challenge you to practice gratitude in how God cares for you individually. You are the beloved. You are seen, heard, and known. We send mixed messages to the heart-head when we have negative feelings about money and provision. Have you heard the old fable "Win the lottery and you'll be bankrupt in a year"? Why is this? In our culture we have movies that depict the wealthy as wicked. In our churches we often deem making money the same as the prosperity gospel. And while we may think with our conscious minds that more money would be good, if the heart-head believes it will cost you your soul, it will be quick to encourage you to get rid of it instead of viewing it as a blessing.

This section's breath prayer is simple. "I am thankful for all the ways I have been provided for. Right now I have everything I need. Right this second I am loved and cared for." This statement is void of greed and lack. It is a peaceful retraining of the mind. What we want is to show the heart-head that an abundance of provision is how we give and receive. It is necessary in our society.

Breathe in and out the gratitude for what you do have, and trust God to provide you with what you need now, tomorrow, and for every occasion. He's very wealthy, and he loves to share.

SECTION EIGHT
Sunny Disposition

DAY 71

Excitable Entries

*Be still, and know
that I am God.*

Psalm 46:10

If your eight-year-old son has symptoms of ADHD or simply can't sit still for more than seven seconds, you might want to steer clear of orange paint. Orange is a stimulating, warm color. Orange represents optimism, enthusiasm, vitality, and creativity.

If you just have to have shades of tangerine in your life, painting your front door orange says a few things about your home and your hopes for your neighborhood. A burst of orange on your front entry indicates joyful hope and potent dynamism. If you paint your door a glossy apricot, your welcoming invitation is unspoken but clear. Most likely any and all folks are welcome at your house. However, if you opt for a rusty or terra-cotta flair, you are probably still generous, but please call before you come over.

Bright oranges, peaches, and warm pigments from the ocher or cadmium groups absorb blue light. This is why terra-cotta pots and cobalt blue marry so flawlessly.

Similar in feel to orange is the warm and welcoming and happy yellow. This sunny color is of the cheery "Hello, neighbor!" kind. Yellow is associated with sunshine, gold, happiness, and prosperity. I love yellow as an accent, and a yellow rose, which is the symbol of wisdom and joy, is my favorite bloom.

Goodness, the complexities of color are unlimited in their potential. And it pains me to acknowledge that some people cannot see color in all its glorious nuance due to color blindness.

The most common form of color blindness is red–green. A person with color blindness could also have problems across the entire color spectrum, influencing not just reds and greens but oranges, purples, pinks, browns, and grays as well. Sometimes even black can be muddled as dark blue or green.

It's a sad place to be in to miss out on the vibrancy of the created world. I could try to describe the heat of the color orange to someone, but if they can't see it for themselves, something is missing.

And it isn't just those who cannot see color that miss out on the brilliance around them. When you look at yourself, what do you see?

Do you see all the sparkling color God painted in your life? Do you see the bright light of happy yellows contrasting with the cooler moments of blue? Do you see the red-hot talent you were gifted with? The inviting orange of the Holy Spirit in you? The purple spark of friendship? Or are you still hiding behind bleak habitual practices of worry?

Take a minute to write down all the strengths God has given you. If you're struggling, take a free online personality test (try Myers-Briggs or Enneagram) and a spiritual-gift inventory. When you have your re-sults, review the list of positive character traits. Now thank God for all the amazing gifts he gave you to do amazing things.

From now on, expect to see all the colors, hues, highlights, and wonders of a life in service to belief.

Wow! The comparison is glaring.

THE FINISHING TOUCH

Father, comparison and trying hard have not served me. I enter into your rest with great expectation to see and experience your bold and daring promises. I can't wait to gaze upon what happens next. Amen.

Eagles, Foxes, and Sun Gods

But those who hope in the LORD will renew their strength.
They will soar on wings like eagles; they will run and not grow weary,
they will walk and not be faint.

ISAIAH 40:31

In winter 2021 I had just finished and turned in my fourth book, *Rest, Girl: A Journey from Exhausted and Stressed to Entirely Blessed*. It had been a hard, long process, and I really believed all would be smooth sailing from then on.

And then I woke up with a crick in my neck.

After several days of discomfort, my mom suggested I visit a chiropractor. During the appointment I was jumped on, twisted, contorted, and cracked. The next morning, I woke in sheer agony. I was not only in more discomfort than previously recorded, but I also couldn't feel or use my right arm.

As an author and artist, my world came to a screeching halt.

At the time of the chiropractic injury, the outline and proposal for this book were already in the competent

hands of my agent. I was terrified that I wouldn't be able to write or illustrate it. I knew of no way to get out of my suffering. My conversations with God—both in my head and in the muffled screams into my memory-foam cervical support pillow—were harsh and desperate for help and healing.

But after several months without relief, void of hope, I figured I was finished. During this time of questioning God and his healing, I was brought back to my original appreciation of Southwest design . . . and worship.

Much of my art has a Southwest folk art twinge. A good portion of my childhood was spent growing up in the mesas of New Mexico. I love everything about the designs of Indigenous people. From the warmth and comfort of fry bread to roughly smooth adobe structures, to the nods to wildlife, nature, and sky, I love Southwest culture and design. There are some who view Indigenous art and culture as witchcraft, and, for a while, I'd stored away my favorite trinkets and collectibles and vowed to neglect anything I might have gleaned from them.

But in the confines of suffering, I wondered about the forgotten obsession and toyed with the idea of witchcraft as a solution to my agonizing predicament.

What? The pain was *really* bad.

In my excruciating stupor, I watched documentaries on Southwestern tribes and their practices. I found comfort in footage of rugged deserts, fragrant cactus blooms, and magenta-and-orange sunsets.

One afternoon while Justin drove me home from a doctor appointment, a fluffy blond fox crossed the road in front of us.

I yelped with delight. Having never seen a fox of such unique color and having never seen a fox of any kind in the Houston area, we reveled in the sighting. But pain, my constant companion, soon drowned out the fox conversation.

When we arrived home, I retired to the recliner as Justin returned from checking the mail. He handed me an envelope. Inside was a beautiful, hand-painted thinking-of-you card. The message on the inside was an offering of prayers and well wishes for my speedy recovery. The image on the outside? A blond fox painted on a scene of desert tranquility with an Indigenous sun symbol and eagle in the upper right corner.

God spoke. He knew. He heard me, and in the jumbled mess of coincidences and hocus pocus, he used a chance fox sighting and a distant friend to remind me that he sees me, hears me, and knows me.

We can assume things about God. We can accuse him of being late, harsh, or unreasonable. But he knows what speaks to us at the exact moment he needs to. And he alone knows every thought that holds us captive to squalor and every prayer that leads us to restoration. In the treachery of suffering, I was met in an intimate way. If we acknowledge these moments of connection, we are teaching the heart-head to look for and expect more of this type of communication.

Do you have a time where you know for sure "That was no coincidence"? Write about it. And then affirm that to the mind with this statement: "Because that cool thing happened, I can expect to see . . ."

Ooooo. Look at you. So brave, talking to God like a personal friend. Attagirl!

THE FINISHING TOUCH

I expect that you know me better than anyone. I expect that you will hear and answer me. While the "shazam" of healed and whole is what I crave, I trust you. I trust and believe. All that you expect of me is faith. All I expect from you is all that you promised. Amen.

DAY 73

Southwest Design

As far as the east is from the west, so far has he
removed our transgressions from us.

PSALM 103:12

The earthy color palettes and old-world accents of Southwestern style remain wildly popular in home planning and decor. Early Spanish settlers brought the cooling architectural aspects of their forefathers' designs to the New World, incorporating them with years of tradition, function, and design from Indigenous culture and craft.

The textile craft of the Southwest continues to inspire and enhance

spaces with geometric and symbolic patterns. In modern design, Southwest bling is often paired with a Mediterranean flair. But back in the day, the early American settlers were welcomed with scorching heat and harsh, sometimes terrifying terrain. They had meager ability to create comfort and were forced to make do with what they had and what they could craft from the severe habitat. Everyday utilitarian items that were the bare minimum—such as cowhide rugs, earthy accents, wooden furniture, and hammered metals—are now key elements in Southwestern style.

Terra-cotta pots, bowls, and vases were handcrafted and hand-painted with symbols of what the Indigenous tenants knew to be true and credited to their survival. Southwest style never cowers in its use of patterns, which is why an eclectic heart such as mine is crazy in love with it. No matter the color, texture, or print, Southwest decor is a stress-free vibe, as it requires no matching and simply feeds off that which you love.

Much like the desert, a color palette of Southwest influence meets with the reds and browns of the native sandy dunes, with tiny pops of turquoise waters, pastel sunsets, and yellow and orange cactus blooms. Masterfully crafted, twisted, and woven baskets in earthy, natural colors and terra-cotta pots that hold cacti or succulents are common in a Southwest design.

While some find the harshness of the West less glamorous, its origins speak of nature and the God of our creation. One of the many common sightings in a Southwest composition is the use of skulls and aged, discarded wooden accents. In its simplicity, I find the expectancy of death—returning to the earth, the dust from which we were formed—a lovely element rarely celebrated in other designs.

We expect that death will come, and celebrating it as a rite of passage is where we meet with humility and a healthy fear. But our spirits will go on and on in union with the God who created us. And living in that union is what we were designed to do. Did you catch that? You were uniquely, individually designed to hang out with God. When God first created the world, he walked with the first people. I imagine a leisurely walk where they talked about the day.

When there are so many people in the world, it's hard to imagine that the keeper of the stars is wholly focused on you. But he is. He'd love nothing more than to go on a walk with you to chew the fat. You don't have to wait for someday to make that happen.

I invite you to stand in the sun sometime this week. If you can do it today, great. Stand outside or in front of a window and look up. Don't look directly at the sun! Geesh. But just acknowledge your friend Jesus. Feel the warmth. Practice being God's attention. Because you are.

THE FINISHING TOUCH

I am ever hopeful for our meeting after my days under the sun, when my wanderings in the harsh terrain of the world have ended and I'll be greeted by you for eternity. I celebrate my time with joy and praise, on earth as it is in heaven. Amen.

DAY 74

A Clever Cabin in the Woods

I can do all things through Christ who strengthens me.

PHILIPPIANS 4:13 NKJV

Before we moved from our big house in town, Justin used his abilities and a few antique odds and ends to build us a little cabin in the woods of our family ranch. With a set budget of a thousand dollars, he used antique doors salvaged from his hometown's movie house, windows from a building he'd renovated, and old barnwood and tin from neighboring scrap piles to craft the niftiest seven hundred square feet of rustic paradise one could fathom. He even used the galvanized metal bucket, the one we'd served sodas from at our wedding, to craft the kitchen sink.

When the theater in Justin's hometown closed, the doors could have been trashed, never to be used again. When the windows needed to be replaced with something more energy efficient, certainly no one would've assumed the old windows had new value.

But what was meant for the dumpster, what seemed worthless and of no use, was transformed. And I am not just bragging about my husband's ninja construction moves. The cabin, with its original intent being an occasional weekend retreat, ended up being our actual home for six months in 2005. I had the bright idea, but Justin agreed, so I am not the only one to blame.

Yes, we had four children under the age of seven. Sure, it would be crowded and most likely exasperating. But we would swap the comfort and luxury of our built-with-our-own-two-hands four-bedroom, three-and-a-half bath, ranch-style home on three acres in town to make a new home by living in seven hundred square feet of semi-sealed, rustic, no-bedrooms, one-bath cabin for almost two hundred days.

Looking back on all that, the building of the cabin and our time there with our children, I am proud of our resourcefulness. It's a story about our abilities, talents we learned from our experiences, passed down for generations. Which, well, sounds pretty boastful, right?

But it is all true. It is the story of limited funds, a young couple, and their not-so-little family. It is a story about recycling, building, dreaming, coping, and design. It is a story about function and livability. And it is a testament.

Over the years, I have found myself in a position to testify. No, not as a lawyer . . . but darn it, I would have been good at that.

Because I can do all things through Christ who strengthens me.

You know that Scripture, right?

You've probably said it a time or two.

But what have you learned from saying it? Did you prove it to the heart-head in a way it could learn from?

Sometimes we water down accomplishments by talking too much about humility. The cabin in the woods was a humble dwelling, but it was a showstopper because of the story behind it. We bucked the idea that new is better and repurposed and celebrated rich history. Things that had been cast aside but were still usable decorated the little space where our family roasted marshmallows and played ten thousand rounds of penny poker. The significance of that little cabin on our family's memories are vast.

Our memories are impacted by those who went before us as well as our own personal histories. We gain wisdom and insight from their craft, and we are warned and advanced from their mistakes.

What do you have behind you that makes all things possible?

God stands behind you—the power of bringing the dead back to life. There's also history—of you overcoming, of your family learning a lesson. Look to the past for inspiration to move through today. Write that story. Brag about what God did. Tell all the tales, leaving out not one of the amazing details. And feel it. Feel that unstoppable truth that is Christ in you. The hope, the glory, and the ability to do anything.

Wow.

You are really something, girl.

THE FINISHING TOUCH

Jesus, I can do all things through you who are my strength.
That's right . . . I mean it. Amen.

DAY 75

Mind Makeover

We've focused on our individuality. At my lowest, when I felt no one understood how much was at stake and the pain couldn't be described, I met with the freedom of knowing I was seen, heard, and known. As much as we've talked about interiors and decorating, I want the next few readings, with their bright colors and nods to rustic Southwest flair, to be an ode to nature. The sun and sky are constant reminders of our creative and loving Father in heaven.

Look up! Look higher. Standing in the sunshine barefoot is even better (if it's not minus twenty degrees). Note the feelings of standing under the open sky and acknowledge, "I see you and you see me." Use it as a breath prayer. Dive into the feelings of nature, and bask in the warmth of his adoration, just for you.

Seated Yellow Retro

*If the LORD delights in us, he will bring us into this land
and give it to us, a land that flows with milk and honey.*

NUMBERS 14:8 ESV

Several years ago we bought an old house as an investment. Initially we were going to use it as a rental. Not long after the purchase, we packed up our clothes, kids, a few odds and ends, and we moved into the house to care for Justin's mother, Iris.

We quickly realized that we wouldn't be able to stay there long. All four of our oldest children were piled into one bedroom with bunk beds. Sam, an infant, had a makeshift nursery in the hall closet. The dining room table we'd had at the ranch seated eighteen and would not fit in the eat-in kitchen of the temporary dwelling. This gave me license to thrift shop.

So one afternoon when Justin could stay with Iris, I went on the hunt for a bargain. I made only one stop. The yellow table for four was staged at the front of the store. It had the original Formica top with chrome trim and legs. The chairs were covered in shiny yellow vinyl. The setting was in immaculate condition.

Among my favorite memories in the care and keeping of Iris are the evenings, after her bath and before dinner. She would sit under the hood of her yellow dryer chair and read gardening magazines while I prepared supper. And then we would crowd around the yellow table and eat dinner together. The children would tell of their day. Iris would ask questions and tell stories. We were squeezed in, but I don't remember feeling choked, stifled, or afraid.

When I look at the yellow dining room set, I can still see Iris enjoying her grandchildren and embracing her time with them.

It makes me think of the things she owned—things that were given to her by God for her to claim. She owned humor. She was funny in a quiet, snarky way. And she owned compassion and empathy, pride in her family and land, and a work ethic that was nothing short of stunning.

Those memories of my mother-in-law are things I own too. They are the precious trinkets of the past. But I am compelled to point out that not everything we say and feel is necessarily a thing we want to own—things like "my worry" or "my stress." Bless my mother-in-law; I can't help but wonder what she would say about this entry. I remember she claimed a lot of things she did not want. Things like "my cancer" and "my horrible luck" were words that rolled off her tongue, as they do many of us. But the fact is that cancer and bad luck are not things she was designed to claim as hers.

This recently came up with one of our children who was struggling with anxiety. He said, "Well, it is because of my anxiety."

I was quick to remind him, "You don't own anxiety—you own peace

[Philippians 4:6–7]. Anxiety is not yours to keep. You may feel anxious, and you may deal with and manage anxiety. I know—sometimes it is hard, and you cope so well."

Similarly, I tease that I was raised in hotels and campgrounds, but it is a disservice to my subconscious to own homelessness as if I was destined for struggle. I was created for peace and provision.

We can acknowledge our past decisions without letting them define us. We can also claim ownership of that which our good God has given us. In fact, God invites us to sit and own our journey and renounce that which is not for us. It might sound like I'm nitpicking. The difference between "I am anxious" and "I deal with anxiety" seems slim. However, the power of our words guides and directs us to the next great find and the expectancy of a bright future.

What a wonderful seat, with a delightful view of bright, sunny days ahead, planned just for you.

Try it today. What are you saying is "mine" that doesn't really belong to you? Remind yourself that stress, anxiety, and discontent aren't part of who you are. Take a deep breath. Now all that is yours is peace.

THE FINISHING TOUCH

Lord, I acknowledge the past and the struggles and triumphs. Thank you that you are always at my side. I give thanks and praise, and I claim gratitude as mine. I shine with the expectancy of a bright and glorious future. Amen.

Tiny Adjustments

*You say, "I am allowed to do anything"—but not everything
is good for you. You say, "I am allowed to do anything"—
but not everything is beneficial.*

1 Corinthians 10:23 nlt

Simple is often associated with stress-free. But a current trend in simplicity is the tiny house, which most would find a challenge. Many of the tiny-home seekers are all about the hippie vibe. They claim they want to "live off the land" or, better, be "off the grid," meaning that they use no government or private cooperative's water or power sources.

For a while I thought this was what we, too, needed in our lives, and lucky for us, I mean me, we had just the right structure to make this dream a reality, right on our very own ranch.

This tiny house on our property, coined "Bob White Hollow" when it was built in 2007, was made from recycled plastic, mud, and more mud and was initially used as a little getaway from the North Dakota–based owner's harsh winters. But as things often do, the marriage between the couple who'd built Bob White Hollow ended, and the off-the-grid orange mud hut at the bottom of a ravine on our ranch sat vacant for several years.

And then in 2015, with three of our eldest out of the house and a new itch for change, I proposed we sell the majority of our belongings and move into the Earthship with the four kids under our roof. I fancied the idea of minimal living, three small rooms, one bath that would definitely need to be converted to on-grid, and the nifty Southwest-style kitchen. My literary agent at the time beamed at the possibilities. One fancy-pants author downgrading from extravagance to meager, tiny living while documenting the transformation on social media, landing a show of my own on HGTV, and all of us collecting the royalties in joyful bliss.

Yeah, the dream was short-lived. Three days into the renovation, Justin called from the hollow, the quails chirping in the distance. "Bob White. Bob White." He was quick to report that he would not be living in the mud hut. Period.

See, Justin had opened a wall between two rooms to find . . . a den of rattlesnakes.

While I expected to have an adventure, Justin had had all the adventure he could muster. And in an instant, tools were packed up, plans were thrown in the trash, and he was home, showered, and committed to city-dwelling, snake-free living.

Just because I had visions of an amazing life in less didn't mean that was what was best for Justin, my kids, or ultimately me.

On day 74, we created feelings around "I can do all things through Christ." But that doesn't mean you have to *do* all the things—some things you are just not called to. Are you taking on things that are simply not for you? While I don't want a rattlesnake den in my would-be pantry, I could have made Bob White Hollow work for me and the kids. However, what would the environment have been like if I had to scrape Justin off the bedroom ceiling every time the foster baby dropped her bottle?

Worrisome at best.

"I can do all things through Christ" does not mean that ignoring someone else's comfort and rest is good for you, especially if the result is stress for both of you. If I project my abilities and inabilities onto someone else and then expect them to respond as I would, we'll all be an anxious mess.

Today's charge is simple—tiny, if you will. You can only decide for you. What is for you and what is not for you is between you and your Creator. When we pick apart the reasons, motives, inabilities, and capabilities of another human, or project our practiced feelings, which are our heart-head beliefs, we add to our frustrations and concerns.

Oh, beloved, this is no tiny thing. We can sort out our worries on paper and identify troubles we are borrowing or projecting.

What worries are not for you? How can you help without owning someone else's reaction? You know what to do—write it all out.

THE FINISHING TOUCH

Lord God, thank you for seeing me and knowing how I roll. I can expect your loving guidance when I make plans and when those plans change. You are my rock and fortress, my personal guidance system for what is mine and that which definitely is not. Thank you for this specific and intentional wisdom. Amen.

Orange You Glad

For I am confident of this very thing, that He who began a good work among you will complete it by the day of Christ Jesus.

PHILIPPIANS 1:6 NASB

How is it that I have two daughters and neither of them can fathom my adoration of pink? When we moved southward from West Texas and purchased our home, the room that would be Sophie's was purple. No worries—that is why the good Lord invented paint. Sophie, who was highly insulted by the blinding lavender walls of her new room, asked if she could paint the room a soft gray with one accent wall.  We were run ragged trying to move out of the mansion on the thirteenth green after the pipes burst in the owner's suite. I said yes without inquiring further.

Justin was traveling back and forth from the ranch, which was still for sale. So my dad gave me the name of a painter. Busy with the new home setup, I gave Sophie, who was fifteen, our paint wheel and told her to tell the painters what she wanted. She toiled over samples while the painters primed the walls with no less than three cans of primer. Early the next morning, they returned with the requested paint color.

At nine the next night, they still hadn't left. They hadn't come downstairs or wandered out to their truck all day. Sophie paced, ready for the reveal and bed. Finally, at 9:30, the painters emerged, insisted there was no charge, and sheepishly sneaked out the back door. We went to her room to investigate and were hit with the heavy smell of cleaning products and the harsh, visual assault of a pumpkin-orange accent wall. Sophie squealed with delight. I cringed and then cringed again when I noticed the carpet beneath the wall was also pumpkin orange.

Yeah, those poor guys spilled the paint on the carpet. The empath in me felt so sad for the stress and worry the two young men must have gone through. The new homeowner in me was like, "Come on, guys." The color of the wall, orange, being an excitable and stimulating color, had my mind spinning. Justin would freak out . . . or not. He knows what it's like to mess up on the job. It happens.

But here is where the paint meets the orange peel—it was of no benefit for me to lose a moment of peace over a piece of orange. There was nothing to be done about it. The bed nicely covered the ruined piece of carpet. I deemed the orange spill no big deal. A few days later, when Justin returned home, I delivered the news.

He looked a little miffed and then said, "Oh well, it's just carpet. I sure hate how stressful that must have been for the painters. I wish they knew us better and knew we just don't worry over stuff like that."

We can unburden ourselves of much angst if we decide not to assume what someone else may say, do, or feel.

We have an entire essay here with

assumptions about the painters' and Justin's feelings and emotions. But really, I only fully understood Justin's response because he spoke his reaction. The painters? I got nothing. But we still hold no blame.

Along with not being able to control spilled paint or the person who spills it, of course I can't make Sophie love another color. So it's my responsibility to deal with and resolve my feelings about Sophie's affection for all things "spiced cider and pumpkin."

As communication becomes faster and more furious, if we don't deal with conflict openly, we are left with unorganized, bothersome spaces that morph into big emotions. Those emotions in turn affect us, because we don't realize how greatly we have let someone else's choices, preferences, or beliefs muss up our mind's walls.

Write it out, baby love. Are you in a place where you think you may have assigned someone else some feelings? Or maybe someone else has spilled their orange paint on your rug. Write to Jesus. Write to yourself. Write to the person you are considering. Resolve your conflicts about that person's preferences and communication (or lack thereof). Be willing to talk to the other person about what's going on. Release your expectations of that person. You can't make them do or say anything. You can only control you. But you can be confident in your Creator and that he will carry you through . . . peaceably.

THE FINISHING TOUCH

Lord, I acknowledge that sometimes I get hot and bothered by the world and its mishaps. But I choose your peace. You clean up the messes and turn mishaps into something wonderful. Amen.

DAY 79

Gratitude and Trust

Let the peace of Christ rule in your hearts, since as members of one body you were called to peace. And be thankful.

COLOSSIANS 3:15

Just down the street from our current home, progress on a new house intrigued our family. As we drove past the new build on our way to and fro, Justin was quick to draw from his construction experience to explain to our two young sons, Sam and Charlie, what was happening at the construction site.

"Look, boys. They just delivered the brick." And "Oh wow! They are making great progress—the roof is finished. The house is in the dry." The boys always asked, "How long until it's a whole house?"

And Justin always said, "It takes about three months." And while this little book, taken day by day, will take about three months to read, I propose that you can profess completion of your restoration project now.

This practice of believing it is finished is a huge step in your remodel.

Whether you have restored or built a house or witnessed others do either, you no doubt know that renovations

232

are a ghastly undertaking. It's a process that takes time and patience. Worse, undoing a mess to create something new usually means the old has to be torn down. But believing as if I have received is a mindset that has completely changed everything for me in every aspect of my life.

Every stress is only made more stressful when we do not truly believe what God tells us in response. Imagine that you hired someone to fix your air conditioner. You made the call, planned for the technician to be allowed into your home, and left instructions for payment. You left for work *knowing* it was going to be a squelching 105 degrees that night.

You need air-conditioning.

What is more stressful? Believing that when you walk in the door you'll be hit with a cool blast of mechanical air because you trusted your efforts? Or worrying that the company you hired might not show up?

I can't promise they'll show up. Honestly, they can't fully promise they'll show up—stuff happens. I can't promise that you won't need a new unit. But I can promise that God shows up, and not only does he have the best in mind for you, he's powerful enough to make it happen.

Are you seeing this more clearly now? Our beliefs are not about wish making and getting precisely what we want when we want it, but believing that God has you cradled in his capable hands.

Oh, darling, this is so relevant in my own life right now. I wish we were together so you could experience the realness of my joy and freedom as I release control to God. At the time of this composition, I have completely stepped away from all social media. Talk about stress. From the beginning of my writing journey, I have been taught that social media is the only way to promote my books.

Really?

That was the question I asked myself. Is subjecting myself to the constant chatter of others' opinions, ugliness, filters, and trolls the only way? Is God not capable?

Hmph.

Getting bogged down by those things is not how I roll. I know that I am seen, heard, and known. And I am so steeped in my beliefs. I have practiced writing and saying them out loud for so long that I am not worried about social media completing the work God and I started. I am wholly focused on what was started in me, and I look forward to how it will be completed. When I believed social media was the only hope, I was hopeless. When I practiced the feelings of God accomplishing his promises, as they apply to me, I experienced rest.

Thank you, Jesus. No hashtag required.

What about you? Write out something that you want to trust God's plan about. Now, what would you say to thank him if that were already accomplished?

Oooo, you sound so sure of yourself, missy!

THE FINISHING TOUCH

Jesus, thank you for helping me with my unbelief. This is where I will experience more of you and less of me. Less of my worries and strife. Help me release the process to you. Give me eyes to see you in the progress you have promised. Thank you. Amen.

Mind Makeover

We often neglect and belittle our individuality, comparing and expecting others to secure our value and place. We compare ourselves and judge others in an effort to feel better about our lives. Instead this comparison game causes stress to the heart-head.

Remember the heart-head is looking out for you. It sees you rehearsing negative things and signals the mind to get out of Dodge.

The good news is that you can soothe it and teach it through the feelings you embrace. If you knew for sure that you alone were the main focus of the God of the universe, why would you look to the right or the left? Continue practicing the feelings of being seen, heard, and known. The Father's adoration and intense care and keeping of you is all yours. Just look up. It is like a game of I spy. Where do you see him? Let him know you see him too! This is such an effective means of stopping judgment and comparison in ourselves. If his image is in everyone and he is in everything, how do you respond to that person or situation?

Let's try something different. Read 1 John 4:9–10 below, filling in the blanks with your own name. Meditate on the words.

"This is how God showed his love [to] _____ : He sent his one and only Son into the world that _____ might live through him. This is love: not that _____ loved God, but that he loved _____ and sent his Son as an atoning sacrifice for _____ sins."

Get back to knowing you are known.

SECTION NINE
Purple Power

DAY 81

Clearly Marked

What may be known about God is plain to them,
because God has made it plain to them.

ROMANS 1:19

E ver spotted a purple front door? Maybe with a beach house or as a festive touch to a midcentury-modern design? But purple, on the whole, is a pretty loud color. However, with the rise of the lavender plant, pops of purple have become more common in home decor trends.

When we first moved our family to the ranch, I asked Justin if we could paint our fence purple like the neighbors. He laughed and said, "Well, I mean, that isn't a decoration." Unbeknownst to me, a purple fence post is the universal sign for no trespassing. Universal? I am part of the universe, and I had never heard of this. But now I know, as do you.

If a fence post painted purple is the universal sign saying NO TRES-PASSING, you know that there are legal and safety ramifications if you do indeed put your lovely feet on the wrong side of that fence.

A man of unlimited adventure might see a purple fence post as a challenge. However, most of the population will just avoid scaling purple fences (assuming they know this is universally understood).

What about you? Are you a fence-scaling kind of human? Or a heed-the-warning kind of human?

See, what we know about ourselves is imperative. Now, as we near the end of our reno project together, I feel so eager to, somehow, cut you loose to wander in elaborate halls of grace.

But I would be remiss if I didn't leave you with the ability to clearly raise your own DO NOT TRESPASS sign.

I have been where you are. Looking over words and images that someone else experienced. I have been in the place where I was hoping, praying that "this time I will get it." And while this is my fourth book, it is my first devotional. Ironically, it's been a little stressful because of the edits. And I am thankful for that. I am grateful that I get to tell you, stress and worry will still come, even to the author and illustrator of a book about stopping stress and worry. But it has allowed me to practice and intentionally learn worry-free living.

The real me must acknowledge the feelings real me has. So the real me is in real panic right now, as my editor approaches these words: "Thank you for allowing me to consider this work. Thank you for clearly marked questions. Thank you for the opportunity to investigate these words' impact on myself before others were invited to consider these ideas for themselves."

Ah, I feel better now. I invite her in because I know she is safe. If she weren't, I wouldn't be able to write vulnerably for you. I would rightfully put up my purple fence and say, "Do not cross."

But where are you right now? What surrounds you? Are you safe? Those words of gratitude to my editor truly soothed me. I needed them as a writer and as a believer in peace.

I want you to mark your

territory. What do you need? Past these ninety days, what borders do you need to put up to protect your peace? What signs will you look for? What will you practice and in turn learn?

In the past, as I have devoured books like these, I have closed the pages only to find myself wishing I was more perfect, a better believer, like the author. So I am posting this sign. I had to be edited, like, a lot. I had to practice all the Mind Makeover methods excessively. And I am weepy— like hair-tussled, snot-flinging, third-day-same-stretchy-pants, purple-hot-wreck *weepy*. Please know that changing your life requires the work of posting signs—I WILL GO HERE; I WILL NOT GO HERE; PLEASE ENTER; NO TRESPASSING.

No one else can tell you anything else, paint it any other way, and make it *yours*.

What do you need to finally finish this project?

Write it out, baby love. Edit yourself. Ask yourself questions about what you are saying.

Just for fun, I recommend writing it in purple!

THE FINISHING TOUCH

Father, help me mark my territory. Help me make peace my own.
Thank you. Amen.

Energy Efficiency

We also pray that you will be strengthened with all his glorious power so you will have all the endurance and patience you need. May you be filled with joy.

COLOSSIANS 1:11 NLT

*E*nergy efficient is a buzzword in our day and age. According to reports, from whatever source, the ice is melting, or we are getting more of it. The sun is still burning, but maybe too hot. The water is running out, but it won't stop raining. Sounds pretty dire.

Your heart-heads ponder the threats even as your curious conscious mind keeps reading and calculating: Is she a lover of polar bears? Wait—was that a pro-life statement, or pro-choice? Is she going to hug a tree? What is happening? And while the conscious part of your brain mulls all the information coming in, the subconscious is still processing the threats, possibly triggering a chemical panic response.

Maybe your hands tingle. Maybe you feel short of breath or the need to move around. Move around? Why? Because that helps you move the chemicals through your body. Because if you were being chased by a lion, you'd need all that adrenaline to give you super speed.

The thing is, there is no lion. The stresses of politics, religion, society, or my beliefs are not physically chasing you. However, since the subconscious can't tell the difference between perception and reality, your feelings trigger the chemicals.

Energy is the feeling behind panic.

I want you to take a big, deep breath of oxygen. Oxygen is the life force that our God gave us to live and breathe. Now take another big, deep breath of the most rampant energy-rich molecule that exists on the planet. And then let it out. Take another big, deep breath and then let your breathing return to normal. When we inhale, air enters our lungs, and oxygen from the air moves from our lungs to our blood. At the same time, carbon dioxide, a waste gas, moves from your blood to the lungs and is exhaled. This natural occurrence is called gas exchange. Oh, and it is essential to life. Oxygen gives you energy that is power instead of panic.

Now before you run from these hippie-sounding words about deep breathing like a kid running from a bloody, knife-wielding clown, what are you feeling about the words you just read? Are you thinking, creating, or receiving?

As you have progressed in your mind renovation, I've asked you to uncover and acknowledge what you are feeling. Feelings are simply the energy of your emotions. And today's exercise is a practice that I do often to tap into the energy and power of the Holy Spirit.

Still unconvinced?

I would like to invite both your subconscious and conscious mind to the following conversation. After you have read the questions, write your answers either in the margins or in a handy notebook.

What do you breathe?

Do you have to think about breathing?

What is oxygen?

Did you know oxygen is energy?

Do you know what oxygen energy produces?

Oxygen energy produces more energy. So is energy bad or good?

What is power?

Do you have the power to google the word *power*? What does *power* mean?

What kind of water heater do you have—electric or gas?

What powers your water heater?

So is power bad?

How do you feel about the words *energy* and *power*?

Energy isn't just about crystal balls or electric bills. As you strive toward a stress-free life, it's normal to feel depleted as you expend enormous amounts of emotional energy on breaking down limited, unhelpful beliefs and organizing your thoughts and reactions. But I also know that it is a lot more energy efficient to not have to worry about something that is of no bother to those of us in Christ. And the good news is that God gives us the Holy Spirit (called the breath of life) and all power. So take a big, energy-filled breath, give yourself some grace, and maybe take a nap too.

Look at you and your energy-conscious self.

THE FINISHING TOUCH

Lord, open my mind. Flood me with fresh energy and new wisdom to fully experience all that you offer me. I love you. Amen.

DAY 83

Grief Decor

Blessed are those who mourn,
for they will be comforted.

MATTHEW 5:4

I f grief were an ocean and you were stuck in it, what would be your goal?
To find an island?

To get out?

To sink or swim?

Often as grief washes over us in waves, we don't know which way is up.

We don't know how deep the ocean of grief is, how far out is too far, or if there is an end, let alone where it is. Were I in the middle of an ocean, I think the thing that would be most eerie is not knowing what lies underneath the water. The mere idea of being attacked from below and not knowing it was coming is my ultimate nightmare. And yet having lost someone's company, having surrendered to the inevitable, knowing I loved well, is enough to keep me treading the waters of a great loss and pressing toward the new normal.

Some might say it is time to climb into the boat and give up, that a loss is just too much. Others might go under.

Oh, but grief is personal. The escape or the staying power cannot be measured in knots, wave height, or depth. In the throes of loss when our foster daughter was removed from our care after two years, I remember details of the journey I would not forsake. Grief takes us on a journey with an indecipherable map—not out of the waters but through them. We cannot accurately plan or decorate for it. It is not measurable now, and I cannot record what saying goodbye might've looked like a month ago or three years ago today.

If I have said it once, I have said it a thousand times—grief is the *celebration* of loss.

Did you catch that? When we lost our foster daughter, I determined that for me, grief was a marked time of *feeling* the loss of a child I loved to be with.

Grief was, and some days still is, a celebration of good things, a reminder that I can have good people in my life, a good career, attend good events, and have a good life. Still, there will be trials. Sometimes things do not turn out the way we thought we would have liked.

Of course, we all move through grief differently. I do not always wallow in the ocean of loss. Today I might just float on my back on the surface and let the tide carry me where it will. But I have come to face grief with a different mindset. I write about grief and let it remind me that I am worthy of the good plan God has for me and my children. I am not lacking in faith or disappointing Jesus when I am underwater in my suffering. Ultimately grief is a reminder that love is worth the risk of the nauseating undertow of loss.

Should anyone tell you that grief isn't Christian, let me remind you that even Jesus wept (John 11:35). Should anyone tell you that your grief is too much, they aren't you. This is not their party. You can cry if you want to.

I propose that we have underlying beliefs about grief that pop up in the nooks and crannies of our heart-heads. Loss is not fun because we were created for growth. Loss is painful because it signifies the absence of that which we enjoyed.

Of course, I cannot know the valley you have walked through or are walking through, so I want you to make this your own. I want you to hear what you are saying and therefore believing about grief.

Our minds are full of thoughts. Some of them are clear, for our benefit. Others are simply rehearsed thoughts, which do not serve us.

Today I invite you to write out some thoughts on grief and then read them out loud. Note if you cry or laugh or even get angry. You are creating a form of communication with your heart-head and God. Ask him to help you direct feelings that don't serve you from feelings that help you. Write out your questions, and express yourself and the experience of loss only you feel. Decorate your personal grief space in what you find soothing and healing.

It is one style of decor no one else can do for you.

THE FINISHING TOUCH

Lord, you are the only one who understands the depth of my losses and my fear of more. I surrender to your healing power and comforting energy. I acknowledge you, my friend. Amen.

Expecting the Finished Work

It is for freedom that Christ has set us free.

GALATIANS 5:1

E very time I'm neck-deep in book composition, Justin is a champ. Scanning art, sorting emails, arranging appointments, home-schooling little boys, and bringing me food as if I were a prison inmate. Then he always sits patiently and listens to me read another four thousand words . . . one last time. When I finish reading a fragrant tale that includes glimpses of our life and growth, I look up from my Mac and say, "Well?" And he says, "It is amazing. I just wish I could be left out of the tales. Can you leave me out?"

Bless him.

I love that man. He couldn't have known when he hauled his nineteen-year-old bride over the threshold of a tiny blue house at that edge of his hometown that she would turn his dreams of a quiet, private existence with half a dozen kids and a few cows into books for the world to see.

But really, he can't be left out.

My husband, who asked to remain anonymous, carried a tired child up the stairs earlier. Later we talked about the long day, and while I wept, he comforted me. He was exhausted, too, but he still found the space to be kind. This is my eleventy-billionth project, and you'd think I would learn that my husband would have my back. But I was still gobsmacked by his gracious response. Out of respect for him, I won't tell you what he said. But trust me when I say that it was really sweet. He treats me like a princess.

Sorry, babe. It doesn't work—you're just too amazing to be left out of my tales.

I feel this way about God's grace. When I write the words I am driven to compose, I find myself telling tale after tale about the phenomenon of the grace of God.

Grace—the gift of freedom and perfect love given through the resurrection of Christ—is too important to our story to be left out. See, we were not meant to be chained to brokenness, deep in the pangs of unworthiness. The Lord brought us out of darkness and broke our chains (Psalm 107:14). Furthermore, he declares us royalty (1 Peter 2:9). Imagine him placing a robe of glorious purple on you.

A life without grace is a life without hope.

Shoog, let's be honest with each other. You and I, we can't get out of our pain, grief, and anxiety alone. We know this. We've seen this. We need Jesus.

But there are times when we fall back into old patterns. We allow the past to creep in again and tell our heart-heads that bad things are coming.

If we let it, grace will step in. Even when we mess up, even when grief and anxiety pull us down again, Jesus holds out his hand. Jesus wants us. He pursues us (Luke 19:10).

I pray you see all of the story. I ask, in Jesus's name, that you will be drawn to the truth and that you won't ignore, modify, or contain Jesus's gift of freedom and belonging.

Some may not like the idea of grace, thinking that too much freedom causes anarchy. Others might say we've lost our minds, pointing out their belief that no one (let alone a powerful God) would let us off scot-free.

But not only is love the story the Bible tells, it's the only story I ever want to tell. God's grace covers us and keeps us in the dry when life's storms batter our house.

Expect to be safe and covered.

Look back over the last few years. When was a time God showed up? Maybe you once prayed over a kiddo who has sensory issues and when you accidentally put her socks on inside out, she discovered they felt good that way. Maybe you missed the application deadline but still got into that program you desperately needed. Maybe you got a call from a friend you haven't heard from in years, and she was just thinking about you when you most needed a friendly voice. Today make a visual reminder of that time you knew and felt God's help—hang a sock on the wall, paint a rock purple, post a picture of your friend—whatever will remind you that God shows up. Go crazy and feel the beauty of his favor and grace. You are God's princess.

THE FINISHING TOUCH

Jesus, I may have missed some parts of the gift of grace, but I expect to now embrace every aspect of my freedom in you. Thank you for treating me as your princess. Amen.

DAY 85

Mind Makeover

You are of noble birth. You are the royal elite. What power this evokes. And is that not the goal? To take back our lives and bask in the promises of Jesus? Go ahead, princess. Write a short story of the romance of your salvation. Leave nothing out. Feel the feelings of the specialness the Father has created in you. He knows you. This is everything in the ways of peace. Write or tell yourself a story through imagery in your mind. Practice feeling the truth of who you are. A daughter who is seen, heard, and known.

Go on—feel that nobility!

The Vanity Chair

But blessed is the one who trusts in the LORD,
whose confidence is in him.

JEREMIAH 17:7

The chair was free, and no one had claimed it. It was the type of odd that slowed traffic but still didn't cause a standstill situation. I passed it twice.

The first time I thought, *Well, that is a weird chair.* And the second, *Really weird.* Then unable to get the homeless chair on the corner of Sayles and South Eighth out of my head, I made a U-turn and brazenly loaded it into my SUV.

When my family saw it, every single one of them asked, "What is it?"

I wasn't sure, so I googled it. "Google, what is a vintage chair with a high back, low seat, upholstered in purple velvet?" The best I can offer is that it is likely a fifties high-back . . . chair. It's not curvy like a Chesterfield, and it's too old to be a nineties gaudy velvet, stiletto-heel chair. But I think that it aspired to be.

While it was ugly, it had something special, kind of like a pug—so ugly it's cute. Besides, it fit perfectly under my vanity table. At first I thought I would re-cover the chair. But upon further investigation, I deemed this well beyond my reupholstery capabilities.

The twenty-three craftily covered and masterfully tufted buttons were the first issue I couldn't conquer. The second was the intricately detailed cording that edged the cushion. The third and final obstacle was the lack of attachments. I turned the chair upside down and sideways and found nowhere on the throne-like seat to take it down to the frame.

This discovery enticed me. I noted the quality. It was impressive. I also noted it was a good seat. Comfortable and supportive. If I were Goldilocks, this would be the chair I would pick. So I decided it was just right . . . after I fumigated it.

Eleven years later, the ugly chair is still, ironically, my vanity chair. As we are on the hunt for a new home, I wonder if it will match with the owners' en suite.

No, it doesn't really match anything. Maybe a better question is this: Will it be tacky or too much?

I don't think so. It is a statement piece.

What is the statement?

It says, "This is who I am. A vanity chair. I have some wrinkles, stains, and wear. But I was created on purpose, with intent. I am bold in my uniqueness, rich in texture, warm in character, and sassy in design."

Perhaps like me, in your quest for peace and rest, you have found yourself trying to be entirely different, more like someone else. From experience I can tell you that effort is a futile and exhausting endeavor. My unique crafty joints were not meant to be dissected but embraced. They are how God created me.

I don't want to be obnoxious, but friend, do you have any idea who you are? All around us are women who are raising their voices and being empowered in their divine creation. This is the kind of equality Jesus fought for. And it means you can do whatever God's called you to.

In order to do that, we have to get our minds organized. We have to audibly and physically list those quirky, unique attributes we know were assigned to us by our Creator. Oh, but we worry. And we rehearse those worries and attach feelings to them. Am I enough? Am I too much? Do I match? Will I be acceptable?

Beloved, you were created on purpose. What is different or special about you? How can you word something you don't like about yourself and flip it? For example, "I am a worrier" feels better as "I am a big thinker. If I don't rein in my thoughts soon, I'll be the next president!" Take control of negative, bothersome thinking by repurposing your words and thinking new thoughts.

Every inch of you was detailed according to he who loves you, knows your potential, and revels in your perfection (Hebrews 10:14). Sure, you might like to see some improvements in your general appearance, but I invite you to stop worrying and start celebrating the you God made. Take a minute to list three things you've thought as negative about yourself. Now, reword those as strengths. Are you too quiet? That might mean you think hard and creatively about situations. Too loud? That means you're enthusiastic. Too emotional? That means you feel deeply and are likely quite empathetic. Too stoic? That means you're someone who is steady and reliable. In a word? You are . . .

Perfect.

THE FINISHING TOUCH

Jesus, I acknowledge my unique creation. Thank you that I am like no other. I give thanks and praise for the craftsmanship and intention that went into my design. I expect to see more of what you see, and I wait with anticipation and great hope for all that you've created me for. I cannot wait to see what I uncover next! Amen.

DAY 87

Mine

Deep in your hearts you know that every
promise of the LORD your God has come true.
Not a single one has failed!

JOSHUA 23:14 NLT

I am confident that Jesus is exactly who he claims.

The peace that statement brings cannot be taken from me or you. Well, in incidents of leaky pipes, stained carpet, and contractors who forgot to show up, peace might feel it's sprinting away. But we can catch peace quickly by reviewing our steps.

The first step is acknowledging, "Yep, this is the pits. However, even the pits are covered by my Jesus." Note the usage of *my Jesus*. By using ownership words such as *my*, the subconscious is alerted to possession—Jesus belongs to me, and I belong to him. Ownership is something the

254

subconscious understands. It has experienced ownership through statements such as *my husband, my house, my car,* or *my kids.*

Next, give thanks. Whether you give those yelps of praise in gratitude that things aren't worse, or you find a reason for the pain, or you find things that have nothing to do with the situation but bring you joy, gratitude is your attitude. And attitude is everything when communicating with the subconscious. When you focus and claim graciousness for all that is going well—the things you love and appreciate—you're no longer focused on the lack or frustration. In turn, the heart-head is now on the hunt for the things you love, which made you feel good, so it can share in the revelry.

Finally, I claim my good expectations. Again, I use possessives, but this time I communicate belief in the things God has promised and declared mine with my verb usage as well. "I *am* so excited to see what happens next! I *am* eager to see *my* Jesus's plans unfold." Within those declarations of anticipation for the wonders and solutions are things I have yet to experience. But when I believe that Jesus has the best in mind for me, a switch flips and I am at rest. Lighthearted living in a snap.

Yeah, I know. The carpet of my mind is still stained with a rim of orange paint. We are master creatures of habit. Even reading the words *breaking habits* alerts the subconscious to trouble. The heart-head likes your habits. They are a fuzzy, warm throw or snuggly quilt that conveys a message of comfort and ease . . . even if they stink like the dog's vomit. But why is that? Because they are yours. "I love my wedding quilt. My grandma made it. It is so soft, and it has all my favorite colors."

If I see my wedding quilt from across the room, my subconscious knows where it came from, why I love it, and my feelings associated with the familiarity. What is the feeling you have when you are in the comforts of familiarity? Or what does your heart-head believe is comfortable? What things have you said for so long, imagined, and felt that the subconscious recognizes as yours?

Yeah, I know—it's a thing.

For years I said, "My thyroid disease." Oh my. I owned

it. I fostered, cared, and fed the pesky affliction. And then it was to blame for incidences of weight gain and weight loss, headache, depression, anxiety, and countless doctor appointments. What's more, it got me out of uncomfortable situations that did not *feel* good. Like dinner at my in-laws' or a movie I didn't want to see. "Sorry. I can't. My thyroid disease is giving me trouble."

I was not created for constant stress or the hormones that followed. Now, I barely acknowledge thyroid issues. Instead I focus on what is working efficiently, and I thank my body for doing so many things perfectly. I listen to my body, and I bless any medication I ingest, specifying what it is for and why. "Bless this medicine to my body. Use it to heal and progress me. It's thyroid medication—please use it to stimulate my thyroid gland." You can call me crazy, but we were told to pray without ceasing, to focus on what is good, and to believe as if we have received. And by golly, I'm going to thank Jesus for working through medication, doctors, and positive reinforcement. My subconscious thanks me for the switch to lighthearted living. Now it's your turn.

Your subconscious is now privy to the power of your words and possessives. Write a list of things you claim as yours. Should they be yours? What is way back in the closet that needs to be hauled to the dumpster? Write it out!

THE FINISHING TOUCH

My God, my Lord and Savior, help me as I progress in the ways of peace. I acknowledge you are good. I give thanks, for you have heard me. I wait in joyful expectation for an answer to my prayer. Amen.

DAY 88

Hollywood Regency

*Let us come before him with thanksgiving
and extol him with music and song.*

PSALM 95:2

Hollywood Regency is an interior design style that grew in fame from the 1920s to the 60s and again since the mid-90s. Hollywood Regency is one of the most ageless yet entertaining interior styles out there. It combines thrilling blends of art-deco-inspired silhouettes and geometric shapes with a mature vibe of high-gloss glamour. Consider regal French furnishings, bold colors, clean lines, and lacquered, reflective touches through purposeful uses of mirrors, crystal, and high-shine surfaces.

Creating a Hollywood Regency interior will require you to implement bold and contrasting colors. If you are a lover of hot pink, rich purples, emerald green, goldenrod, turquoise, black, white, and blood-orange red, this style might be your jam.

Much like the real Hollywood, when it comes to a Hollywood Regency color palette, the rules are fluid. The goal? Be bright and stand out. Shiny whites and sleek blacks are secondary to the pops of accent colors, creating a loud contrast that exudes confidence.

And there it is. Confidence, the beast lurking in our heart-head asking hard questions and giving harder, nearly irreverent answers. We had the confidence of a loved princess in the beginning. I mean, we roared onto the earthly scene confident we would be cared for.

Then came comparison, where we learn we either have too much confidence or not enough.

However, there is no scientific means to know how much is the right amount of confidence. The lack of useful measuring tools leads us to attempt to define appropriate levels of confidence through subjective judgments. Unfortunately, as we've already learned, judgment of others is actually a comparative judgment of ourselves. If we accuse a sister of being overconfident, then we are deeming ourselves less. If we accuse her of having no confidence, then we are judging ourselves as having more or enough.

All that comparison is exhausting and terrifying and "do I have enough bling in my room to be cool, or does it just come off as trying too hard?"

I have to tell you some insider information, straight off the red carpet. This is hot news. Ready?

You are doing just fine.

You are not too much—you are not, not enough.

You are exactly where you need to be right at this moment. You are not missing out or barely making it. You are adored, seen, heard, and notoriously known as God's beloved royal purple child.

And you are so highly esteemed, you can expect to receive more of Jesus and experience more highfalutin glamour because he holds you in such high acclaim.

Don't believe me? The Bible says God knit you together and you are wonderfully made (Psalm 139:13–14).

You are chosen (1 Peter 2:9). You have a job that God prepared for you before you were born (Ephesians 2:10). And you are loved lavishly (1 John 3:1).

It's not greedy or selfish or clingy to acknowledge a proper confidence in God or who God made you to be. It is, in fact, exactly what God wants for you and what you can expect when you realize that he adores you. Write out the list of hot news from above. Read them out loud to yourself, and accept the truth in them. Now readjust how you measure yourself using God's true measurements.

Look at you, Hollywood, so sparkly!

THE FINISHING TOUCH

How great you are my God and love. I wait with joyful anticipation for the next amazing guidance from you. I expect your kingdom because you said I could. Amen.

DAY 89

Move-In Ready

*Finally, be strong in the Lord and
in his mighty power.*

Ephesians 6:10

I guess it's that time. The last day of a huge project is always bitter-sweet. In the beginning, there is the vision. And then in the end, there is the big reveal. While I've imagined us sitting together over tea and cake in some fancy room with views of rolling greens and soaring blue skies, I don't get to see the results of your mind renovation.

But I trust in the God who is with you now and always.

I'd like to leave you to consider staging. In house sales and renovation television, there is a process where the home is staged to show its potential. It is helpful. Sometimes seeing how someone uses a space helps us envision how we might use it. And I hope I have set a stage that allows you to envision your life worry-free.

The funny thing about staging is, it is only for show. It does look amazing. But, girl, you and I both know we are not setting our tables with bow-tied linen napkins and vases of fresh grapes. Staging has value, but function is what we crave.

Really, as much as I would love to *shazam* your mind into the freedom of tangible belief, all I have done is set the stage. If my stage is decorated with too much light and way too much essential oil, that won't work for you. I will only speak for myself, but I suspect you will identify. This has to be yours. You and Jesus. Your space to think, create, and receive. No one else can do it for you.

This is the best of what I have left. Take a seat. Pick a comfortable spot, one where you can clear your mind and listen. I know you are busy. And I know sometimes worry and stress rage onto the scene without considering where you sit. Still, I implore you, take a seat.

When your mind is running in circles and your body is pumped full of stress hormones and angst, imagine Jesus. Picture him patting a huge purple throne right next to him.

He'll look at you and say, "You are different. You may not feel different at this moment, but you've done amazing work in redecorating your heart-head with good positive ideas and words. Now all that is left to do is sit. Sit and speak truth to yourself. Sit with me. Sit with me and tell me all that delights your soul. Will you do that?"

Can you see his kind eyes? Can you see the strength in the hands that made you for a purpose? Can you see the scars there from his sacrifice? Trust him now, and snuggle up on that royal chair.

Tell him that you see him and feel him.

Go on now, tell him.

And do it again. The more you do this, the more the subconscious will agree and believe in the practice.

Then give thanks. Thank him for the ten toes you have or the nine you have left. But in everything give thanks. Then just sit in joyful expectation. Maybe turn on some praise music and sing along. Claim the promises inside the lyrics as your right. Expectation is a sign of certainty. It is a nod to knowing for sure that you are seen, heard, and known.

As you adjust to your new carefree way of living and being, your subconscious will get comfortable with the new way too. And soon it'll have no interest in ever going back.

How do I know? Because once you are free, you are free indeed. The old has gone, the new has come . . . seated right there with you.

THE FINISHING TOUCH

Lord God, thank you for these eighty-nine days. Let them be a part of my life as a mark of my transformation to live happily ever after in my newly renovated space. In Jesus's name. Amen.

Mind Makeover

Say it with me now: I am a new creation in Christ.

Yes. You are.

Thank you for joining me on this renovation project. I pray it blesses you and holds you tightly in every season. Think through the various practices we've looked at over the last few months. Which one was most beneficial to you? Commit to keeping that practice up.

Friend, it looks just perfect!

Jesus be all over your beautifully refurbished self.

Love,
Jami

Acknowledgments

Thank you, Jesus—you are my friend.

To Justin—sorry, babe. I told stories about you. I love you and I like you.

To Maggie, Christian, John, Anne, Luke, Sophie, Sam, and Charlie—I love you and I like you. Thank you for being my humans.

To Daddy—thank you for the adventures.

To Mom—I would be without words without you.

To Stacey, Dean, Michael, Kelly, the vandals, and the pixies—I love you each.

To Katie M. Reid—thank you for your unrelenting creativity and cocreating with my wild brain. We are a good team. Daily you inspire and motivate me. I like you.

To Carey Scott—you make me laugh, think, and love better. I think you are pretty amazing.

To Blakely Bering—you have no idea the impact of inspiration and hope you have brought to me. You are a visionary and fresh-eyed wizard.

To my literary agent, Dave Schroeder—I appreciate you so much. I look forward to working with you on the next project and the next and the next . . . I know . . . stay focused. You have changed everything, and I cannot thank you enough. Jesus be all over you.

To Lorraine Reep—you are the epitome of grace and wisdom. Thank you.

To Jeane Burgess—your friendship and belief in my work have brought me to this place. Thank you for your excellence. I love you always.

And to the many friends who have continued to walk with me, encourage me, and love me—Kim Phelan, Marcy Toppert, Susannah B. Lewis, Emily Potter, Shelby Spear, Christine Carter, Michelle Hedrick,

Tracy Steel, Alexa Carlton, Sarah Bennet, Tammy Hardin, and Kandy Chimento, and all my friends, in real life and the cyber world.

To Sandstone Chiropractic—you saved my life. This work would not be possible without your mercy and care. Thank you.

And to Kregel Publications—that was fun. Thank you for this opportunity to share a message in word and color. I have learned more about my work, myself, and my God through the course of this project. It was a pleasure to be in your company. May it be well with you each and all, and may the Lord continue to nourish and advance you.

Notes

1. Andrew Farley, "God in a Swivel Chair?," The Grace Message with Dr. Andrew Farley, April 4, 2017, YouTube video, https://www.youtube .com/watch?v=en23jDN-du4.
2. "Chata," Bible Study Tools, accessed June 15, 2022, https://www.bible studytools.com/lexicons/hebrew/nas/chata.html.
3. Frank Lloyd Wright, as quoted in Mayor Rus, "Step Inside This Meticulously Restored Midcentury Modern Masterpiece," *Architectural Digest*, November 18, 2020, https://www.admiddleeast.com /architecture-interiors/architecture/step-inside-this-meticulously -restored-midcentury-modern-masterpiece.
4. Crystal Raypole, "How to Hack Your Hormones for a Better Mood," healthline.com, July 26, 2022, https://www.healthline.com/health /happy-hormone.
5. Teresa of Ávila, *Santa Teresa de Ávila Complete Works*, 2nd ed. (Washington, DC: ICS Publications, 1987), 447, https://archive .org/details/SantaTeresaDeAvilaWorksComplete/page/n3/mode /2up?q=love+turns.
6. Shigeo Kinomura et al., "Activation by Attention of the Human Reticular Formation and Thalamic Intralaminar Nuclei," *Science* 271, no. 5248 (January 1996): 512–515, https://doi.org/10.1126 /science.271.5248.512.
7. Linda Roszak Burton, "The Neuroscience of Gratitude," Wharton Health Care Management Alumni Association, October 2016, https:// www.whartonhealthcare.org/the_neuroscience_of_gratitude.
8. Christophe André, "Proper Breathing Brings Better Health," *Scientific American*, January 15, 2019, https://www.scientificamerican.com /article/proper-breathing-brings-better-health.

9. Voltaire, *Le Sottisier* (Librarie des bibliophiles, 1880), as quoted in Britannica online, s.v., "What Did Voltaire Contribute to the Enlightenment?," accessed June 20, 2022, https://www.britannica.com /biography/Voltaire.

About the Author

Jami Amerine is an author, artist, mom, wife, and much more. She and her husband, Justin, have six children ages eight to twenty-six, including two boys adopted from foster care. While Jami and Justin have always made their living in construction, Jami has found that one of her callings is writing. Her previous books include *Stolen Jesus*; *Sacred Ground, Sticky Floors*; *Well, Girl*; and *Rest, Girl*, all of which are available wherever books are sold.

Jami is also a successful artist whose work is sold in HomeGoods and other national resellers. Jami holds a bachelor's degree in family and consumer sciences from Abilene Christian University and a master's of education in counseling and human development from Hardin-Simmons University, and is happy to be able to translate what she's learned to help women everywhere.

Learn more about Jami at JamiAmerine.com.